DESIGN LIKE A GIRL

30 groundbreaking women architects and designers throughout history

featuring foundations in design

Written and Illustrated by Sarah Bischoff
Featured Illustrators Yianna Buterbaugh, Lindsey Arthur and Ashyln Young
Portraits illustrated by Endicott College Interior Designers

Design Like a Girl: 30 groundbreaking women architects and designers throughout history
Including Foundations in Design

Printed in the United States of America
First Printing, 2023

Written by Sarah Bischoff
Illustrations by Sarah Bischoff, Ashlyn Young, Yianna Buterbaugh and Lindsey Arthur
Portrait Illustrations by Paige Liljegren, Madison Pelletier, Gianna D'Aprile, Sara Nobes, Kaitlin Desbiens, Amber Vuilleumier, Samantha Eisenbud, Aleksandra Tsangarides, Michaela Ellison, Isabel Davern, Julia Ferraro, Madison Demberg, Sydney Kimball, Jessica Dubois, Emily Shaw, Maeve Kelly, Jillian Hersey and Lauren Bower

ISBN 979-8-2181893-6-5 Hardcover

Published by 13seats
www.13seatsproductions.com

to my daughter Mia you inspire me each and every day, continue to believe in yourself.

to all my family and friends, thank you for believing in me being your wife, stepmom, daughter, sister and friend is a gift.

to all the girls, you are worthy and powerful. I believe in you.

WHO, WHAT & WHY

My story of design started over 35 years ago. As a child I used grid paper to map out my dream house floor plans. I loved dollhouses and redecorating my room. I loved doing anything creative, I made home movies, prepared skits and plays and even started small craft businesses. I was active in sports and theater. I loved being around friends and even got along with my older brother from time to time. After high school I attended Colby College in Waterville Maine, what I believe is one of the most beautiful places in the world. Small school, small classes, it was the right spot for me. My passion for learning about people and continuing my creativity lead me to a major in sociology with a minor in studio art. My friendships were reaching milestones, my brother was one of my best friends and my parents gave me the gift of travel and opportunity. After college I still wasn't sure who I wanted to be. I worked in after-school education for a couple years. Curious of what else was out there I thought back to my childhood passions and decided to see what architecture was all about. I landed a job as an administrative assistant at Flansburgh Associates. I valued the structure of the corporate world that embraced peoples individuality. It was the year 2000 and "interior design" was a brand-new term, at that point there were architects and interior decorators. This was my ah-ha moment, as an interior designer I could merge my love of sociology and art. The study of society and the spaces they inhabit. Driven by excitement, I applied to a graduate interior design program. Upon my acceptance I hit another roadblock. Was I ready for this? I knew this was the career I wanted but the idea of committing to it felt so permanent. I wanted one last moment of freedom. I packed up and moved to Sydney Australia for a year. I waitressed, camper-vanned the coast, jumped out of a plane and had the adventure of a lifetime. When I returned home, I started my path towards my master's degree in interior design. The path had its twists and turns, but all the while I loved what I was doing. I was happy to be up all hours of the night working through design problems. My final year at New England School of Art and Design I studied nonconformity and the roles that we play in our lives. I wanted to challenge the expected through design. This was a true culmination of my love for sociology and design. After graduate school I was fortunate to spend my first couple years with two inspiring women in design. The women of Parker Torres design invited me in as their third employee as they set on the journey to start their own firm after 20 years in the industry. Their guidance and support led me to my next job. I spent eight years building a second family as a retail designer for Bergmeyer Associates. I never expected to be a professor and teach. An opportunity found me and since 2012 I have been able to share my passion and immerse myself in the amazing creative brains of students. In that time I became a mother, stepmother, wife, watching my kids explore their individual creativity is inspiring. I was blessed with female role models in my life from my mom to my professors to my friends and my colleagues. As a professor I take my role very seriously. Although women have been remarkable role models and change makers in the world of architecture and design for centuries, their names have been masked behind men and omitted from the pages of our history books. Architecture and design textbooks continue to celebrate the accomplishments of men throughout time. Occasionally the name of a woman appears, sharing her contribution to the field or highlighting her as the muse of a male architect. These women's stories are not told. Gender and racial inequality in the workplace have been evident throughout history; this book is meant to shed light on the presence of diverse women in design and their impact on our built community.

I am committed to participating, learning and leading.

table of contents

icons

 architect

 interior designer

 residential design

 advocate for women

 education design

 gender equality

 commercial design

 minority in design

 public design

 lgbtq in design

 hospitality design

 environmental steward

 healthcare design

 inclusion in design

*these icons can be found under the story of each woman

TIMELINE OF THE 30 GROUNDBREAKING ARCHITEC

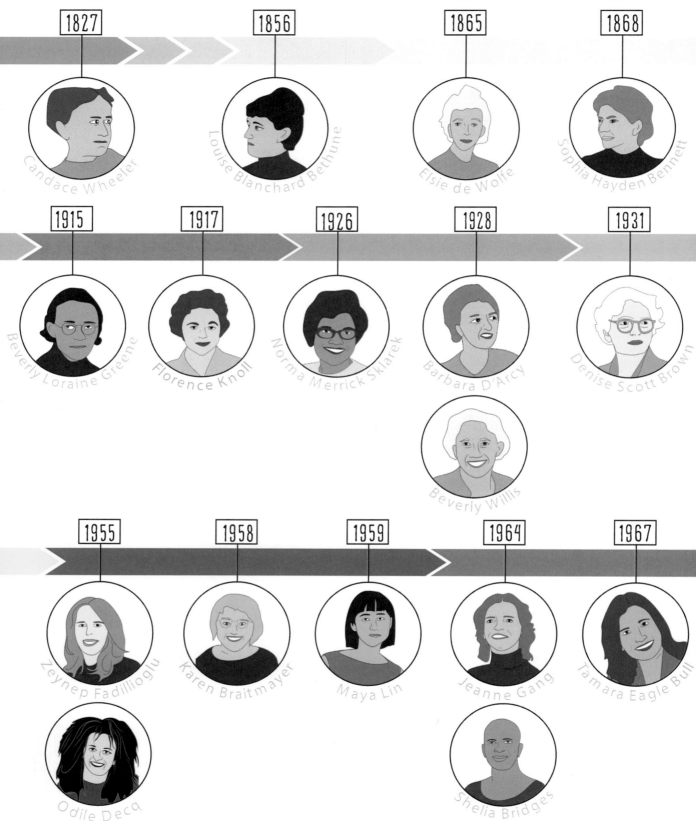

1827 — Candace Wheeler
1856 — Louise Blanchard Bethune
1865 — Elsie de Wolfe
1868 — Sophia Hayden Bennett

1915 — Beverly Loraine Greene
1917 — Florence Knoll
1926 — Norma Merrick Sklarek
1928 — Barbara D'Arcy
1931 — Denise Scott Brown

Beverly Willis

1955 — Zeynep Fadillioglu
1958 — Karen Braitmayer
1959 — Maya Lin
1964 — Jeanne Gang
1967 — Tamara Eagle Bull

Odile Decq

Shelia Bridges

INTERIOR DESIGNERS THROUGHOUT HISTORY

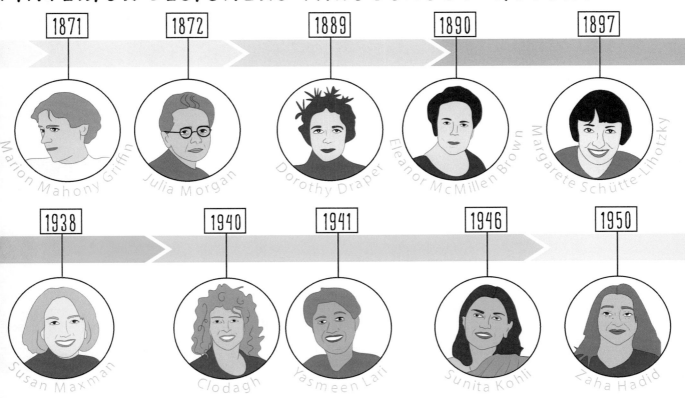

1871 — Marion Mahony Griffin
1872 — Julia Morgan
1889 — Dorothy Draper
1890 — Eleanor McMillen Brown
1897 — Margarete Schütte-Lihotzky

1938 — Susan Maxman
1940 — Clodagh
1941 — Yasmeen Lari
1946 — Sunita Kohli
1950 — Zaha Hadid

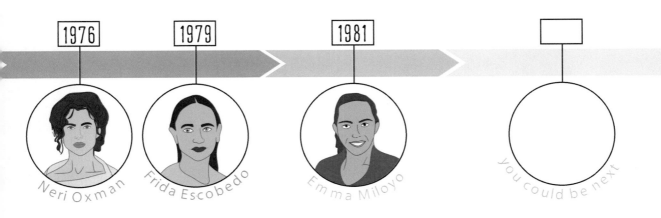

1976 — Neri Oxman
1979 — Frida Escobedo
1981 — Emma Miloyo
you could be next

NORTH AMERICA

SOUTH AMERICA

CALIFORNIA
San Francisco - Julia Morgan
CONNECTICUT
Darien - Karen Braitmayer
ILLINOIS
Belvedere - Jeanne Gang
Chicago - Beverly Loraine Greene
& Marion Mahony Griffin
MICHIGAN
Saginaw - Florence Knoll
MISSOURI
Saint Louis - Eleanor McMillen Brown
NEW YORK
Buffalo - Louise Blanchard Bethune
Delhi - Candace Wheeler
New York City - Barbara D' Arcy, Dorthy Draper,
Norma Merrick Sklarek & Elsie De Wolf
OHIO
Athens - Maya Lin
Columbus - Susan Maxman
OKLAHOMA
Tulsa - Beverly Willis
PENNSYLVANIA
Philadelphia - Sheila Bridges
SOUTH DAKOTA
McLaughlin - Tamara Eagle Bull

AUSTRIA
Vienna - Margarete Schutte-Lihotzky
FRANCE
Laval - Odile Decq
IRELAND
Galway - Clodagh

CHILE
Santiago - Sophia Hayden Bennett
MEXICO
Mexico City - Frida Escobedo

EUROPE

ASIA

RICA

IRAQ
Baghdad - Zaha Hadid
ISRAEL
Haifa - Neri Oxman
PAKISTAN
Punjab - Sunita Kohli & Yasmeen Lari
TURKEY
Istanbul - Zeynep Fadillioglu

KENYA
Nairobi - Emma Miloyo
ZAMBIA
Nkana - Denise Scott Brown

AUSTRALIA

Introduction to Architecture

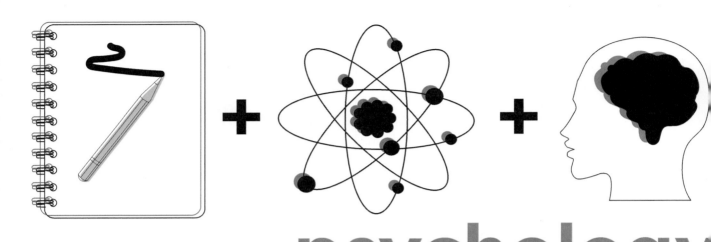

psychology

creativity

technology

community

human behavior

innovation

nd Interior Design

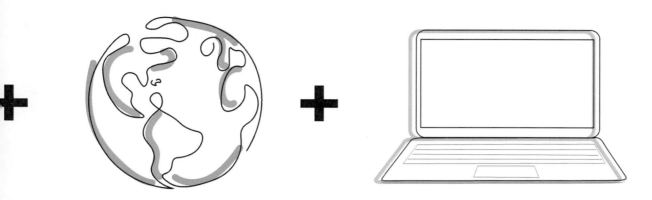

+

+

sociology

sustainability

responsible

art

wellness

science

global awareness

architects

exterior of a building

building site

roofs

facade

exterior walls

collaboration

inclusion

universal design

all phases of design

lighting

building systems

education + experience + examination = LICENSURE

UNITED GOAL IS THE HEALTH

interior designers

interior of a building

furniture

interior walls

finishes

space planning

creativity

communication

ethics

ADA standards

client meetings

budget

building codes

construction drawings

education + experience + examination = LICENSURE

SAFETY AND WELLNESS OF ALL USERS

EDUCATION

High Schools

Middle Schools

Universities

Colleges

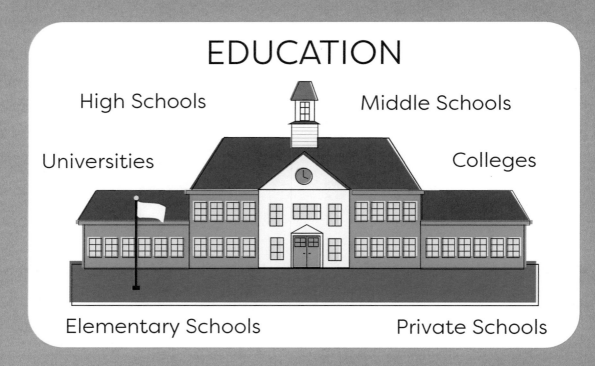

Elementary Schools

Private Schools

RESIDENTIAL

Houses

Affordable Housing

Apartments

Multi-Family Housing

HOSPITALITY

Hotels

Restaurants

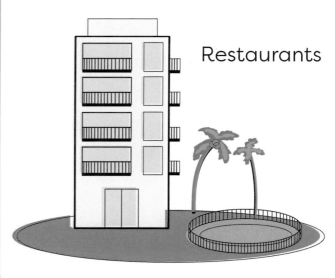

DESIGN

HEALTHCARE

Hospitals

Medical Offices

Clinics

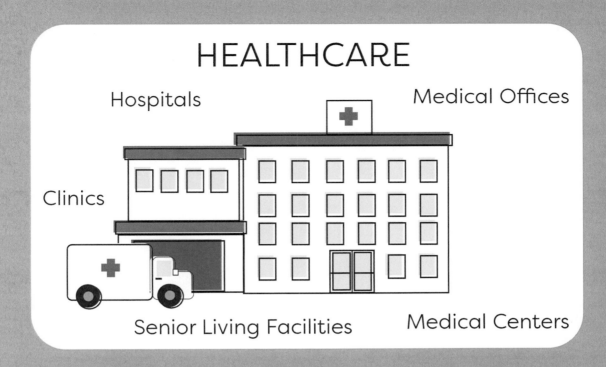

Senior Living Facilities

Medical Centers

COMMERCIAL

Retail Spaces

Banks

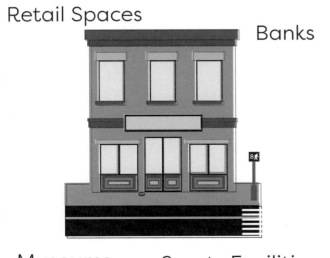

Museums

Sports Facilities

Workplaces

PUBLIC

Government buildings

Libraries

City Halls

Post Offices

Police and Fire Stations

Candace Wheeler

Candace grew up on a farm in Delhi, New York. She was raised in a Puritan household; the Bible was the only book she was allowed to read. Her father was an abolitionist and would not permit his family to use anything made by a slave. Candace and her eight siblings had to work hard to provide all the things their family needed. Candace became a very skilled needlepoint artist. During the time Candace grew up, society expected women to get married and take care of their homes.

At the age of 17, Candace married Tom Wheeler, and with her husband's support she wanted to be more than a homemaker. At this time, it was unusual for women to work outside their home and was only acceptable if they dedicated their time to charity work. Candace could see the need in her community to help less fortunate women and she became passionate about creating opportunities for women to gain confidence and become financially independent. Just like Candace, many women were talented artists and craftspeople. In 1877 Candace co-founded the Society for Decorative Arts. This organization helped women make a career in art and design. Within a year, there were 30 branches of her organization across America. Candace did not stop there, as her passion continued to grow. She also started the New York Exchange for Women's Work, which was a market where women could sell goods they made. Women wanted to work and be independent!

Candace began her interior design work alongside Louis Comfort Tiffany, the well known stained glass artist and designer. Her work included redecorating the White House and designing the interiors of Mark Twain's home. With her determination ignited, Candace started her design firm Associated Artists, where she employed many women. Candace quickly become the most well-known textile designer and interior designer of her time.

Candace continued to pursue many incredible accomplishments. She started an artist colony in New York with her brother that was a safe place where single women could live and create art and support themselves. She believed a woman should not need a husband in order to make her place in society and determine her worth.

Candace became a leader for women, a role model. She not only inspired women to pursue their own careers, but she also gave them opportunities to support themselves financially. She nurtured women, held their hands, and raised them up; she gave birth to career opportunities in art and design for many women. Candace Wheeler was indeed the "Mother of Interior Design."

Louise Blanchard Bethune 1856-1913

Louise was born an only child to Dalson and Emma Blanchard. Her parents were educators and she was home-schooled until she was 11 years old, completing her schooling in Buffalo, New York. Early on, she had her eyes set on architecture. At age 20, she began working as an architect's apprentice. Just five years later, in 1881, she took a brave leap and started her own architecture firm. A fellow apprentice, Robert Bethune, joined her practice. Soon after, they were married, becoming co-owners of Bethune & Bethune. Louise is recognized as the first American woman to work as a professional architect.

Buffalo New York was seeing prosperity and growth at this time; with the Erie Canal open, trade and business were thriving. Louise and Robert contributed by building the new landscape of Buffalo; together they designed 18 schools and many other buildings. In 1888 Louise was the first woman admitted to the American Institute of Architects (AIA), 31 years after its inception. AIA is an organization that was developed to promote architects and architecture throughout America. Louise was conscious of her position in the field and was determined to give women a name in the industry. She wanted to encourage women to be architects and was an advocate for co-educational instruction in architecture schools across the country. Equity in education and the workplace was a driving force for Louise.

In 1891 she was offered an opportunity of a lifetime when she was asked to submit a design into the competition for the Women's Building at the World's Columbian Exposition. While this would have given her astounding recognition throughout the country and certainly put her name on the map, she opted out. She declined as a way to protest the fact that historically, women who won this competition were paid $1,000 for their designs while men were awarded $10,000 for the same achievement. This decision did not stop Louise from continuing to make a name for women in architecture and design. In 1902 she was granted the greatest commission of her career, the Hotel Lafayette in Buffalo. Which today holds a treasured spot on the National Register of Historic Places. The Hotel Lafayette was a place of opulence and grandeur. It was one of the first hotels with cold and hot water in all of the bathrooms.

Louise was a champion for gender equality in architecture. When Louise died in 1913, there were 50 female architects that were following in her footsteps.

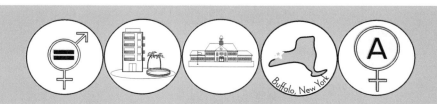

PHASES OF DESIGN

SCHEMATIC DESIGN (SD)

Information gathering
Client research
Project schedule and budget
Site analysis
Concept development
Bubble and block diagrams
Ideation sketches
Programming

DESIGN DEVELOPMENT (DD)

Space planning
Furniture, finishes and
equipment (FF&E)
3D drawings
Code analysis
Perspectives
Custom design elements

1 + 2 + 3 + 4

CONSTRUCTION DOCUMENTS (CD)

Computer drawings
Specifications
Schedules
Electrical drawings
Reflected ceiling plans
Floor plans
Elevations
Sections

CONSTRUCTION ADMINISTRATION (CA)

Permitting
Site visits
Building
Installation
Certificate of Occupancy

"I'm going to make everything around me beautiful – that will be my life."

Elsie de Wolfe

Elsie de Wolfe

Elsie de Wolfe was the life of the party and the sunshine in an otherwise dreary room. Elsie started her career as an actress and soon became more interested in set design and fashion, which sparked her interest in interior decorating. Elsie grew up during the era of Victorian design. Homes were filled with excessive decoration and often lacking in function. Rooms were finished in dark tones, filled with woodwork and patterned wallpaper, carpet and upholstery. One of her earliest memories is when her mother redecorated the family sitting room and Elsie simply could not take any more darkness and right there she threw a tantrum.

In 1886 Elsie and Elisabeth Marbury began what would be a 40 year relationship. Two women who had promising careers and were openly gay was quite notable at the time. In 1892 Elsie and her partner Elisabeth moved into their first home together in New York City. Elsie redecorated their home, moving away from the dark design of the past and adding light and freshness. Elsie was inspired by her summers spent in France and wanted to bring the brightness of the outdoors into her spaces. They hosted parties and teas with the friends and celebrities. Her interior design style was admired by their guests. In 1903 Elsie left her career as an actress and set off to become America's first professional decorator. Propelled by the love and support of Elisabeth, Elsie had business cards drawn up and was on her way. Just two years after launching her business, Elsie received her first major commission. She was asked to design the interiors of the Colony Club, a premier women's social club in New York City. As Elsie describes her work "I opened the doors and windows of America and let the air and sunshine in." Elsie added light colors and mirrors, and made use of bold and colorful chintz fabric, a must-have in upper-class homes. Her free spirit was literally a breath of fresh air for women and for interior design.

In 1913 Elsie published her first book, The House in Good Taste. In her book she shared design advice and her thoughts on what was considered style at the time. Elsie wrote, "You will express yourself in your home whether you want to or not…Its only requirements were to recognize suitability, simplicity and proportion"—that was what she considered good taste. Elsie believed in arranging furniture to promote conversation. She detested the idea of dining rooms encouraging people to spend their mealtime outside among nature.

Later in life, Elsie married Sir Charles Mendl, enjoying a platonic relationship where she continued to fill her life with the parties she was happy to host as Lady Mendl. While women in America were already decorating their homes, Elsie made a profession of her passion and this inspired many women to follow.

Sophia Hayden Bennett   1868-1953

Sophia was born in Santiago, Chile in 1868. Her parents dream for her was to have a strong educational foundation. At age six, Sophia was sent to live with her grandparents in Boston, Massachusetts. Sophia attended West Roxbury High School and continued her college education at Massachusetts Institute of Technology (MIT). Sophia was the very first woman to receive a degree in architecture from MIT in 1890 and she did it with honors! Sophia was one of only 24 women at the entire college. Sophia made quite an architectural impact while she was in college. Her final project was a design for the Museum of Fine Arts in Boston. Her design was inspired by the Italian Renaissance with intricate detailing. Not only did she consider the variety of arts that would be represented in the space she also considered the modern needs of a building including a basement and room for building systems like heating and ventilation.

While her admittance to and graduation from MIT were groundbreaking, finding a job in architecture was difficult for Sophia. It was very much a male-dominated profession where women were not taken seriously. Sophia began teaching technical drawing at a Boston grammar school. Her big break came in 1891 at the age of 23. Sophia saw an advertisement for a competition to design the Woman's Building for the World's Columbian Exposition in Chicago. From a group of 13 entrants, Sophia won! Her design was inspired by her classical Beaux Arts thesis project she had done for the Museum of Fine Arts while in college. Even though this achievement was monumental, the next two years tested her stamina and will. Sophia was paid $1,000 to complete the building design and implementation. If a male architect had won this competition, he would have been paid $10,000 for his work, a gross inequity based on gender that was all too common for female architects in this era.

This job proved to be more work than young Sophia had ever known. During the design process they were continually making changes and even added a third floor to this 80,000-square-foot building, all the while maintaining her insufficient compensation. Sophia worked day and night and suffered from great exhaustion. With all her might she pushed through and was awarded the Artistic Medal at the Exposition. Sadly, this impressive building was Sophia's one and only architectural project. After the exposition Sophia returned to Boston, was married and led a quiet life alongside her husband.

Sophia's accomplishment as a female architect led the way for other women to take chances and it also highlighted the inequality between female architects and male architects. Her career was short lived because of her treatment, but the bravery she had was a gift to women architects

Marion Mahony Griffin   1871-1961

At a young age, Marion and her family had a heroic escape from the Great Chicago Fire of 1871 and built a new home in the country outside of Chicago. Shortly thereafter, her family suffered a great loss; when Marion was 11 years old her father passed away. Marion's mom, Clara, was now a single mother to five young children. Chased by bad luck, their family home caught fire and Clara moved her family back to the city. Through their challenges, Marion's mom was a strong and devoted role model to her children. She was determined to care for her children and became a school principal and was also very active in her community advocating for women's rights and a member of the Chicago Woman's Club.

Fueled by her mother's tenacity, Marion pursued an education in architecture and was the second woman to graduate from Massachusetts Institute of Technology in 1894. Her global curiosity led her to travel to Europe after graduation. When Marion returned to Chicago, she started a drafting job downtown. It just so happens that the company she worked for was in the same building as world renown architect, Frank Lloyd Wright's office. She met Frank early on in his career and was hired by Wright as his very first employee. Marion worked for Wright for the next 15 years. In that time she became the first woman to receive her architecture license in the state of Illinois. Not only was she an accomplished architect, she was also a true artist. Marion changed the way architectural designs were presented to clients. She became well known for her beautiful watercolor renderings and hand drawings of their architecture designs. Her delicate handwork, and meticulous attention to detail brought the designs to life. Presenting these realistic drawings to clients was a game changer in the field of design. The ability for an architect to share their vision before the design was complete was also a great benefit to clients.

During her time at Wright's office, Marion became known for her witty and charismatic personality. She spent her days working on her own designs as well as collaborating with Wright. She became dear friends with Frank and his first wife, Catherine. After Wright's failed marriage and the dissolution of their friendship, Marion moved to Australia with her husband, Walter. Walter had won a competition to design the country's new capital. Marion was proud to collaborate with her husband and talk design from dusk to dawn together. Marion had a long career in design and not only was a strong role model for women but she turned architecture designs into artwork.

Elements and Principles of Design

The elements and principles of design are guidelines to help you make design decisions. An architect or designer applies them to create a well-designed space or building. Consider these as a foundation in your design tool box.

> **Elements are** what **is used to make up a design**

> **Principles are** how **those elements are used**

There are 7 elements of design
and 5 principles

The elements are what make up the space or building. Use the elements as building blocks to create your design.

COLOR

TEXTURE

FORM

LIGHT

PATTERN

LINE

SPACE

The goal is to use the elements in harmony with each other by applying the principles of design.

RHYTHM

SCALE/PROPORTION

BALANCE

EMPHASIS

HARMONY

ELEMENTS

LINE

line guides your eye

horizontal lines create a sense of stability and can be seen as formal

vertical lines show strength and bring attention to height

dynamic lines have energy and movement

SPACE

positive space
(space filled with an object)

negative space
(empty space)

negative space
(empty space)

positive space
(space filled with an object)

COLOR

Color defines mood and perception, how we feel and understand space. Color can be used to make spaces feel: larger or smaller, calm or active warm or cool.

science + psychology

FORM

3 dimensional shape
adds volume to the design

geometric: straight lines

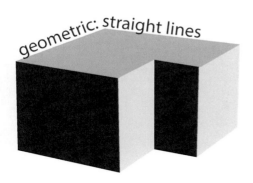

organic: curved lines

TEXTURE

visual texture (2D)
tactile texture (3D)

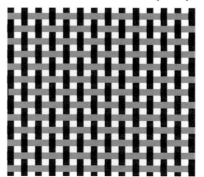

LIGHT

natural and artificial

PATTERN

A pattern is created by the use of a repetitive design. It can add dimension, energy and interest.

PRINCIPLES The sense of experiencing
right. This is because of the principles that have

BALANCE
creates a sense of equilibrium

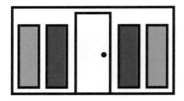 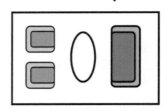 

symmetrical balance
space is evenly mirrored
can appear more formal

asymmetrical balance
space is not mirrored
but still feels balanced
by shape and proportion
can appear more dynamic

radial balance
central focal point
with elements
radiating around it

RHYTHM
A visual repetition of the elements of design. An organization of elements that make the space interesting and encourages the viewer to explore.

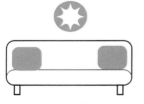 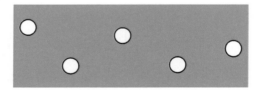 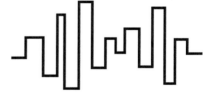

rhythm with color   **rhythm with shape**   **rhythm with line**

EMPHASIS
Emphasis is creating a focal point or a moment of focus. This can show hierarchy, or the importance in the design, highlighting something of interest. Emphasis can be created by any element. It tells the viewers where to look or what to pay attention to.

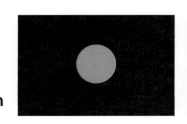

a building or walking into a space and it just feels
been applied to the elements to create the space.

HARMONY

When elements work together to have a pleasing effect. Too much harmony can be boring. Use the right amount to create a sense of calm and stability and engaging environment.

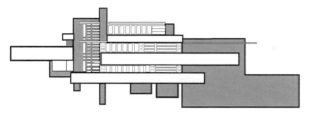

using similar shapes to create harmony

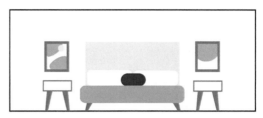

using color to create harmony with different shapes and cool colors

SCALE and PROPORTION

scale: how the element fits into the design
proportion: how the elements fit together in the design

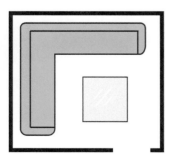

small spaces should not have only big shapes

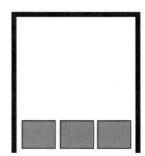

tall spaces should not have only small shapes

scale can be used to accentuate its importance

How elements of a building relate to each other and how the building relates to its site or location. How the elements relate to the human scale of the users of the space. Variation is important but you have to see the greater whole. Scale and proportion must be intentional and have meaning.

Julia Morgan   1872-1957

7OO buildings over 50 years; that is 15 buildings a year! Julia Morgan's designs left a stunning legacy across her home state of California. Julia was born in 1872 in San Francisco and became one of the first women to study civil engineering at the University of California Berkeley. There she was mentored by her professor and well-known architect Bernard Maybeck. After seeing her talent, he encouraged her to study at the Ecole des Beaux-Arts, a world-renowned architecture school in Paris.

At the age of 26, Julia committed to study for the entrance exams while learning French. She was the first woman to pass the entrance exams and not only that, she did it on her first try, something that many men had failed to accomplish. In 1902 she returned to California, to pursue her dreams and did not look back. Just two years later she began her own architecture firm and soon became the first woman architect licensed in the state of California. Tragedy struck San Francisco in 1906 when a devastating earthquake hit, leveling more than 28,000 buildings and flattening the landscape of the beautiful city. Fires burned for four days and many people lost their lives. As the city dusted off from the wreckage, there was much rebuilding that needed to be done. Among the splintered building remains stood the 72-foot El Campanil bell tower on the campus of Mills College. With Julia's engineering background, she had designed this tower with reinforced concrete and its strength withstood the astonishing quake. This design feat did not go unnoticed; the owners of the destroyed Fairmont Hotel defied expectations and hired Julia, a woman, to redesign their hotel.

Julia continued to study the qualities of concrete as a building material and led the way for groundbreaking construction techniques in the field of architecture. Not long into her career she was introduced to the Hearst family, with whom she worked for the next 25 years, designing a variety of projects from the Herald Examiner Building to family homes, including the well-known Hearst Castle. She was known as a client's architect. She embodied their needs and designed buildings and spaces to their style, preference and even fanciful ideas. Julia was never interested in the press, she preferred to work long and hard and was happy to not be interviewed and to avoid the spotlight.

Her portfolio is a timeline of contrasting design styles and building types; she could do it all. It was only after her passing did she receive the acknowledgment that her career deserved. In 2014 she was awarded the Gold Medal from AIA, it's highest honor. Her engineering innovations changed the landscape of design. Not only has Julia left us with a legacy of architectural gems her work will stand the test of time and the challenges of nature.

Dorothy Draper
1889-1969

Dorothy was born into an affluent family in the wealthy community of Tuxedo Park, New York. She led the glamorous lifestyle of a debutante, a young woman in upper-class society. Dorothy dreamt of bright colors and vibrant patterns. Her first decorating project was her family home. Shortly after the design was completed, the family sold their home and the buyer purchased it all, including the furniture and décor.

Dorothy was the life of the party and her style was undeniable. At the age of 23, Dorothy married Dr. Dan Draper, personal doctor to President Franklin D. Roosevelt. Eleanor Roosevelt and Dorothy were good friends and neighbors. Dorothy and Dan had three children together during their marriage. Dorothy was a true believer in design's direct effect on one's happiness. She pushed the neutral and gloomy colors of the past aside for bright greens, reds and pinks. An early adopter of the psychological effects of color on our mood, she was revolutionizing the connection between design and mental health, living by her motto, "your home is the backdrop of your life, whether it is a palace or a one-room apartment." Her designs were the talk of the Manhattan's Upper West Side. Dorothy threw lavish parties and many admired her style.

Dorothy started her own design business in 1925. The Architectural Clearing House connected architects and women who were looking to renovate and update their homes. As Dorothy's popularity grew, she was challenged by the fact that some people weren't ready to adopt her bold style in their homes. She turned to resorts and hotels, bringing her striking blend of patterns, mirrors, checkered floors and vibrant colors to the public. In 1939 she published a book called <u>Decorating Is Fun</u>, to share her wisdom and give courage to other housewives to decorate their spaces with things that made them feel good. Her unrelenting strength and positive thinking carried her through the hardship of a disloyal husband and a divorce. She changed her company name to Dorothy Draper Incorporated, going by "DD" to her clients. She took on projects such as the Carlyle Hotel, the Greenbrier Hotel, and the Hampshire House. Dorothy's work at the Greenbrier earned her the hightest fee ever paid to a decorator. Her old Hollywood style and modernized Baroque designs were like no other. Dorothy's designs were iconic and upon entering a space you would know it was a Dorothy Draper design. She was unique and one of a kind.

Dorothy's legacy continues to this day. Her company is still in business, holding true to her style and zest for life.

SCIENCE + PSYCHOLOGY =

PRIMARY COLORS
cannot be mixed from other colors

COLOR WHEEL
first discovered by Sir Isaac Newton

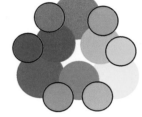

SECONDARY COLORS
mixing primary colors

TERTIARY COLORS
mixing primary and secondary colors

| **HUE** | **SATURATION** | **TINT** | **SHADE** | **VALUE** |
| color | intensity of color | adding white | adding black | light to dark |

HOW WE PERCEIVE COLOR: Warm and Cool Colors

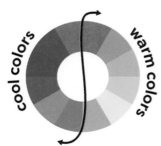

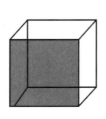

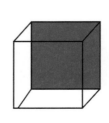

colors have a temperature warm colors like the sun and fire, cool colors like ice and the night sky

warm colors appear to advance

cool colors appear to recede

check out how the colors bounce. Do the warm colors appear to jump out?

COLOR THEORY

COLOR HARMONIES

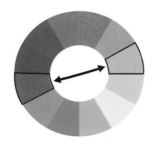

COMPLIMENTARY
colors that are opposite of each other making a harmonious contrast

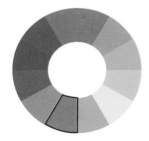

MONOCHROME
variation of one color

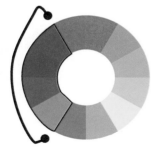

ANALOGOUS
3-4 colors next to each other creating natural harmony

COLOR PSYCHOLOGY

how colors impac

RED
passion
energy
strength
power
determination

ORANGE
creativity
success
enthusiasm
warmth
excitement

YELLOW
joy
attention
fresh
optimism
hope

PINK
compassion
sweet
sincerity
innocence
love

BLACK
power
formality
mystery
rebellion
elegance

GRAY
knowledge
authority
dignity
timeless
practical

sometimes colors in one culture mean something different to another culture

RED:
Western culture: love, passion and danger
Eastern culture: luck, happiness, wedding, new year
Middle Eastern cultures: danger, caution and evil
South African culture: sacrifice and mourning
Latin American culture: represents religion when it's paired with white

color psychology comes from color theory
it is the use of different hues, saturation and the perception of color

our mood and behavior

GREEN
growth
health
nature
harmony
healing

BLUE
trust
sadness
loyalty
calm
stability

PURPLE
royal
luxury
wisdom
ambition
spirituality

BROWN
nature
dependability
rugged
trustworthy
simple

WHITE
clean
simplicity
innocence
honest
purity

use blue in an office
to increase productivity
use green in a bedroom
for tranquility
use yellow in a kitchen
to give you energy
use red as an accent
color to draw attention,
but not to overwhelm

BLUE
lowers
blood
pressure

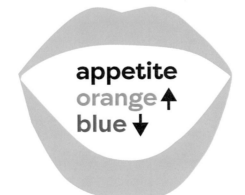

appetite
orange ↑
blue ↓

red =
danger

Eleanor McMillen Brown 1890-1991

It is no surprise that Eleanor McMillen started the oldest interior design firm operating in America today. Eleanor was raised in St. Louis and made her way to New York City. She earned her design degree at the Parsons School in New York and also completed business and secretary school. She had the forethought to see that if she wanted her own business, it would be wise to learn all aspects of the industry. After she completed her education she invested $13,000 of her own money to open an office on the East Side. She named her firm McMillen Inc. instead of Eleanor McMillen, she did not want her firm to face the stigma of a female led company. She wanted to avoid being considered "one of the ladies." Eleanor was courageous for going out on her own, as many female designers worked from home at that time. At McMillen Inc. she believed in higher education and solely hired graduates from Parsons. Eleanor was a keen designer and businesswoman. She beautifully blended antique furniture with more modern pieces and was known for her ability to place furniture and accessories with balance and harmony.

Eleanor was an avid traveler and was married twice. She drew design inspirations from her travels abroad. Eleanor especially appreciated French furniture, which she incorporated into her designs. She also imported and sold furniture from France, introducing her clients to French designers that may not have been well known in America. She completed a range of design projects, from wealthy homes to government properties. She decorated President Johnson's private quarters in the White House. Her unwaivering courage, determination and business know-how proved to be her strength. Clients were not turned off by a woman-owned business because McMillen Inc. proved itself time and time again.

Her legacy is long and proud. McMillen Inc. will celebrate 100 years in 2024. She created a company that withstood the downturn of the Great Depression and flourished. By the end of World War II McMillen Inc. was considered the most well-known residential interior design firm in America. Her design firm was not like any other woman-owned firm of her era. Her degrees in business and design gave her the ability to build a full-service company. She had a design and drafting department as well as a business office. Employees at McMillen Inc. rarely left, as she created an environment that was productive and fulfilling. Eleanor wanted to do it all and she believed in herself and her employees.

In 2014 Eleanor McMillen Brown died at the age of 100. Her dedication and passion brought her to her office every day until she was 85 years old.

Margarete Schütte-Lihotzky 1897-2000

A rebel and an activist, Margarete fought for those who may not have had a voice and designed for those who were not treated equally. Margarete pushed boundaries all her life. In 1915, she was the first female student at Kunstgewerbeschule, University of Applied Arts in Vienna Austria, where she studied architecture. While in school, it became her calling to address the inequities of housing for working-class people who made less money and were not able to afford much. Affordable housing offered through the government or by businesses for their workers, was often lacking in space and inspiration. She was upset by the quality and absence of design that went into their homes. Margarete began her work in the New Frankfurt project, an affordable public housing program in Frankfurt Germany that began in 1924. She was committed to helping to resolve the city's housing shortage.

In 1926 she created the Frankfurt Kitchen, her greatest contribution to interior design. Although she was not known for her cooking skills, she designed a kitchen for the working class that was put in over 10,000 homes. These working class families did not have a staff to cook for them, so it was time to design a kitchen that worked for the modern housewife. Margarete did extensive research and created a mock-up of a kitchen in an old railroad dining car. There she was able to watch women cook and study the process. She watched them move through the space and get the necessary utensils and ingredients for a meal from start to finish. In her "housewives laboratory," she was able to design a kitchen in a small space that focused on comfort and efficiency. While Margarete believed that the traditional roles of the housewife would be evolving as more women joined the workforce, she still believed a well-designed kitchen on a budget would streamline the process of cooking for the family.

Margarete traveled with her husband throughout Europe, helping to resolve design challenges for cities when it came to housing shortages and social housing, housing that was rented to people with low incomes and in turn did not make any profit. She pursued her activism as a resistance fighter against National Socialism, the beliefs of the Nazi party. She participated in peace and women's movements. Margarete declared she "was more than a kitchen" and wanted to make a name for herself as an advocate for her beliefs. During the war Austria became part of Hitler's Germany and antisemitism was widespread in Vienna. Margarete's protesting and commitment to her beliefs lead her to be captured by the Gestapo and they sent her to a prison camp until World War II ended. She was freed by US soldiers in 1945. Margarete returned to Vienna and was treated as an outcast due to her political beliefs. Over time, Vienna's attitude evolved and Margarete was recognized for her peace efforts as well as her architectural achievements.

Vienna, Austria

Beverly Loraine Greene 1915-1957

Beverly accomplished more in her short career than many can dream of in a lifetime. Beverly was met with gender and racial barriers throughout her life but she never gave up. Beverly was born in 1915 in Chicago, Illinois, the only child of James and Vera Greene. Education played a major role in her journey to becoming the first known African American licensed architect in the United States.

Beverly first earned her degree in Architectural Engineering at University of Illinois, the start of her trailblazing accomplishments. She was the first African American woman to receive a Bachelor of Science degree there and she went on to receive a Master of Science degree in city planning and housing. Upon graduation, Beverly was hired by the Chicago Housing Authority, which had not seen many women or minorities on its employee roster up until that point. At just 27 years old, Beverly became a licensed architect in the state of Illinois. Held back by the racial prejudices in Chicago, she was unable to further her career. Architecture firms in Chicago were not open to hiring minorities.

In 1945, three years after receiving her license, Beverly picked up and moved to New York City, in search of more opportunities. She found a job with the Metropolitan Life Insurance Company to work on the new housing development in Stuyvesant. Beverly Greene, a black female architect, would be working on a project that promised better living conditions for New Yorkers and a better quality of life. The site was a former over populated housing disrtict. The new project would reduce the density of people and add more green space for playgrounds and parks. Ironcally, it was a housing complex where African Americans were not allowed to live, this did not go unnoticed to Beverly. This project later became the battleground of an important desegregation ruling in favor of allowing black families to move into the area, four years after it was completed. Beverly did not stay on to see the completion of the Stuyvesant Town housing complex. She left shortly after accepting a scholarship to study urban planning at Columbia University, earning a second master's degree, this time a Master of Art in Architecture. Beverly's career blossomed and she worked on projects with well-known architects of the time. Some of those projects included the arts complex at Sarah Lawrence College, the UNESCO Headquarters in Paris with Marcel Breuer and projects at New York University.

Beverly's groundbreaking career of firsts came to a sudden stop at the young age of 41. In 1957, Beverly Loraine Greene died suddenly after an illness. Her funeral was held at the Unity Funeral Home, a building she designed. Leaving a legacy like no other, Beverly opened doors and broke down barriers for women of color who dreamed the dream of becoming an architect.

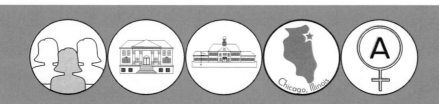

Florence Knoll 1917-2019

Born in 1917 in Saginaw, Michigan, Florence was an only child. Her father died when she was five and at the young age of 12 she was orphaned after her mother passed away. Left to the care of a family friend, Florence attended boarding school. Early on she showed interest in architecture and joined the Cranbrook Academy of Art. At Cranbrook Florence became dear friends with Eliel Saarinen, a well known Finnish architect, and his family. With this family bond, she had the privilege of working beside some of the most famous architects of the 20th century, including Walter Gropius, Marcel Breuer and Ludwig Mies van der Rohe. Her passions led her to study architecture at Columbia University, the Architectural Association in London and the Armour Institute of Chicago, earning her degree in architecture in 1941.

After college Florence moved to New York City. Despite her architecture degree, she was hired into the interior design department. Outside of her job, she began working with Hans Knoll, a German-born man from a well-known furniture-making family. In 1943 Florence began working for Hans full-time as the interiors specialist. With Florence on board, Knoll was headed in an upward direction. In 1946 Hans and Florence founded Knoll Associates Inc., fell in love and were married that same year. They opened their first furniture factory in 1950. Their prediction that modern furniture would be the next trend after the war was spot on. Florence created the Knoll Planning Unit, which revolutionized postwar corporate office interiors. She studied space planning, efficiency and the corporate culture. Florence was the pioneer of a new way of design thinking. She brought together the elements and principles of design combined with human factors and the study of how the spaces were used. Her designs enhanced worker productivity and well-being, and bonded the office community. She worked with well-known furniture designers bringing their pieces to her showrooms and designed furniture pieces of her own.

In 1947 she began a textile division at Knoll. She collaborated with women designers from Europe and America who had developed innovative textile manufacturing techniques. These women were celebrated as visionaries of Knoll Textiles. The furniture division also brought designs from overseas and America to the forefront of postwar design. She was a true curator, collaborating with well-known designers, with both their designs and hers becoming iconic pieces in history. A great tragedy occurred in 1955 when Hans was killed in a car accident. Florence used all her strength through her grieving to take over and lead Knoll Associates to be one of the most well-known furniture and design firms of our time.

INEQUALITY in

48% in 2018
of all accredidted architecture degrees were earned by women

25% ● ○ ○ ○
1 in 4 are females in 2019
of US architects are women

0.2%
of architects are African American women

25.7% 2021
members of the American Institute of Architects, are women

2 of 39 by 2023
Pritzker Prize "Nobel Prize of Architecture"recipients are women, since est. in 1979

timeline

1857
American Institute of Architects (AIA) founded

1992
first woman president of AIA

2024
first African American woman president of AIA

female registered architects globally
1958 1%
1988 4%
1999 13.5%
2005 16%
2020 17%

Architecture

 Finland was the first country to permit women to study architecture

1970's
Women's movement

Title IX in 1972 forbade sex discrimination in any educational program that received federal funding.

1972 women architect organizations and task forces began to form

Conferences addressing women in architecture surged in 1974

1980's backlash on feminism slowed the progression

out of 1,152 women across the globe

would not encourage a woman to start a career in architecture

men earn **18%** more than female counterparts

72% claim to have experienced sexual discrimination, harassment or victimization on the job

Women made **$0.85** to every **$1.00** men make in 2020
the same gap since 2011

Why?

Lack of female mentors

Stigma of powerful and successful women

Lack of equality

women in education
|||||||||| deans
||||||||||||||||||| assist./assoc. deans
||||||||||||||| directors & chairs
|| department heads

Norma Sklarek   1926-2012

Born in New York City's Harlem neighborhood, Norma was the only child of her parents, who were immigrants from Trinidad. Norma was academically inclined; as a child she attended predominantly white schools, including the highly selective Hunter College High School. Norma made her mark early on, becoming the first African American woman to graduate from the prestigious Columbia University with a Bachelor's degree in Architecture. In 1954 she passed her architecture licensing exams on the first try and became the very first African American women to be a licensed architect in New York. Even with her accomplishments at the young age of 26, Norma did not have an easy road ahead. She was rejected 19 times at job interviews, not knowing which was working against her most, being a woman or being a minority.

In 1959 Norma was the first African American member of the American Institute of Architects (AIA). She had to continue push through race and gender barriers in her career. Her break into architecture came with the high-profile firm Skidmore, Owings and Merrill. Early on in her profession, she was kept behind the scenes to hide from clients that there was a black woman working on their projects. After four years Norma ventured west, where she became the first African American female licensed architect in California. She worked for 20 years as director eventually becoming the first female vice president of an architectural firm. She played a critical role in many prestigious projects, including the Fox Plaza in San Francisco, the US Embassy in Tokyo, and Terminal One at Los Angeles International Airport. Unfortunately, like many women architects at that time, Norma was not always noted as the architect of the project. Often her name was hidden behind that of a man, but not for long!

While Norma was thriving in her career, she was married and divorced twice and had two children that she raised as a single mother. In 1980 Norma became the first woman to be elected to the AIA College of Fellows, AIA's highest membership honor. It was just five years later when the female co-owned architecture firm Siegal Sklarek Diamond was established and Norma was the first Black woman to co-own an architecture firm. Those three women took their firm on a journey, becoming the largest female-owned architecture firm with a portfolio of impressive projects in Southern California, ranging from education to public and commercial projects. Norma grew up at a time when she had no professional role models to look up to. The most important of all her "firsts" was becoming that role model for girls and girls of color.

Barbara D'Arcy

1928-2012

Up until the 1950s, most people were hiring architects and designers to create the vision for interior spaces. There was not much knowledge available on how to create your own dream interior. This all changed when Barbara D'Arcy joined the scene.

Barbara was born in New York to an art teacher mother and a moving company manager father. They spent their free time as a family strolling the streets of Manhattan, popping in and out of antique shops. Her love for art continued as she earned her degree at the College of New Rochelle in 1952. Her first job out of college was as a junior decorator at Bloomingdale's department store. Bloomingdale's was the fashion destination in New York City. The store took up a whole city block and was visited by people from all over the country and even the world. Barbara worked in the fabric department and redefined how people shopped for fabrics and furniture. She set up little vignettes or scenes with the furniture pieces and showed she had a true skill for visual merchandising.

During this time Bloomingdale's was going through an expansion from fashion clothing to fashion for the home. Barbara's vignettes slowly turned into entire room designs also known as showrooms or model rooms. In 1958 Barbara was named the chief designer. Her model rooms were a sought-after life-size exhibit, bringing customers from far and wide to see her new designs. People looked to her to find out what was in style; she was a true trendsetter. This was the first time interior design was available to the masses. They could visit and imagine buying pieces of furniture for their own home.

Barbara took risks with her designs and created spaces that were unexpected and often completely out of the box. If a customer didn't leave Bloomingdale's with a piece of furniture, they left realizing that lavender and orange really could go together. She also took risks on other designers, bringing in furniture from overseas to highlight in her showrooms.

Barbara's originality and zest for design was not only recognized in her model rooms; she also redesigned the Bloomingdale's store. Barbara was the first known female retail designer. In 1975 she became the Vice President of Bloomingdale's. Barbara traveled the world, finding inspiration in every nook and cranny of life. She was dedicated to her passion of interior design, retiring in 1995 after 43 years at Bloomingdale's. Barbara changed the way society viewed design because she made it accessible and inspiring. Who knows how many people felt confident enough to design their own spaces after touring the Bloomingdale's model rooms!

Beverly Willis

1928

It is hard to image it's possible to accomplish all that Beverly Willis has in her career. Her childhood was challenging. She was born in 1928 in Tulsa, Oklahoma, and was just six years old when her parents divorced and her father disappeared. Her mother struggled to make ends meet and ultimately sent her and her brother to live in an orphanage. With the job opportunities World War II provided, her mother was able to get her children back. Struggle and survival pulsed through her veins. Beverly took night classes in woodworking and volunteered for the Civil Air Patrol, earning the title of lieutenant. She began her path of higher education at Oregon State Universisty studying aeronautical engineering and after two years left to work in Portland. She soon found herself in San Francisco exploring her creativity in the arts, eventually landing at the University of Hawaii to earn her Bachelor of Arts degree. Without formal training as an architect, she successfully built a groundbreaking career as an architect on the West Coast.

She came across many challenges as an architect. One of her early projects was to design a home for a client who used a wheelchair. In 1960 there were not yet any Americans with Disabilities Act guidelines to follow, so she had to create her own. She studied her client's needs and widened doorways, lowered counter tops, light switches and doorknobs. In 1963 she embarked on a project to convert three Victorian buildings in San Francisco into a retail and restaurant complex, known today as the Union Street Shops. Credited with uncovering another architectural necessity, Beverly did one of the first adaptive reuse architectural projects and inspired a national wave of the desire to restore old buildings. Even with this experience, she was not permitted to sit for the architectural exams without her formal degree in architecture. With the backing and support of Hawaii's Senator Daniel Inouye and California's Governor Pat Brown, she earned her license in 1966.

Beverly started her own architecture firm and has continued to contribute to the architecture landscape we know today. She and her team developed the first computer technology to aid in her practice. An advocate and role model for women, Barbara was the first woman president of the California Council of the AIA and the first female chair of the Federal Construction Council of the National Academy of Sciences. She brought women together to form Women's Forum West, helping women with career opportunities. In 2002 she founded the Beverly Willis Architecture Foundation to bring women to the forefront of architecture, restoring women in the history or architecture. Her truth, ambition and success will forever be a legacy.

History of Architecture

Byzantine

400-600

Gothic

1100-1450

Classical

850 BC-476 AD

Mesopotamian

4000 BC-400 AD

Islamic

700-1000

Renaissance

1400-1600

Early Christian and Midieval

373-500

and Interior Design

American Colonial

1600-1780

Rococo

1650-1750

Neoclassical/Federalist

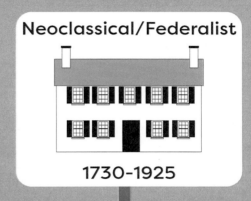

1730-1925

Baroque

1600-1830

Georgian

1720-1800

Greek Revival

1790-1850

VICTORIAN 1837-1900

REVIVAL PERIOD DURING THE REIGN OF QUEEN VICTORIA

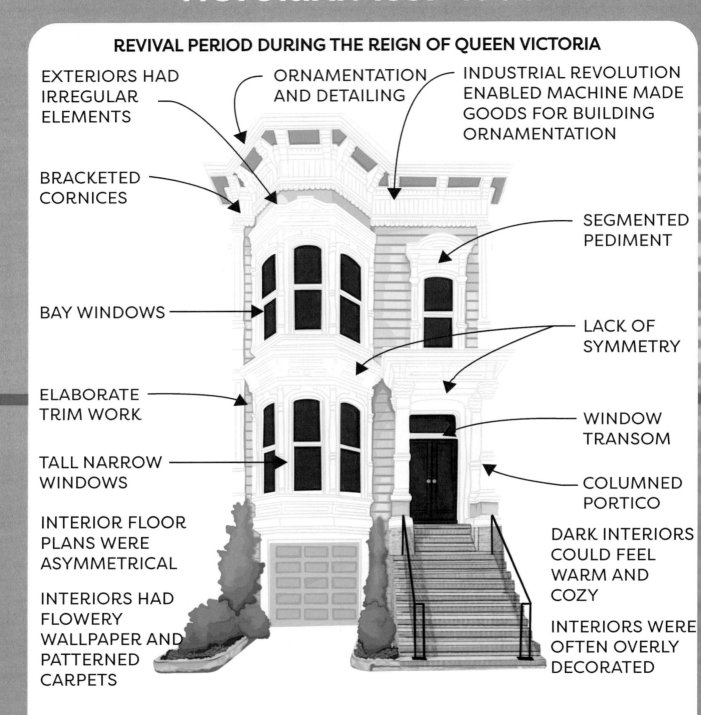

EXTERIORS HAD IRREGULAR ELEMENTS

ORNAMENTATION AND DETAILING

INDUSTRIAL REVOLUTION ENABLED MACHINE MADE GOODS FOR BUILDING ORNAMENTATION

BRACKETED CORNICES

SEGMENTED PEDIMENT

BAY WINDOWS

LACK OF SYMMETRY

ELABORATE TRIM WORK

WINDOW TRANSOM

TALL NARROW WINDOWS

COLUMNED PORTICO

INTERIOR FLOOR PLANS WERE ASYMMETRICAL

DARK INTERIORS COULD FEEL WARM AND COZY

INTERIORS HAD FLOWERY WALLPAPER AND PATTERNED CARPETS

INTERIORS WERE OFTEN OVERLY DECORATED

THIS IS THE ICONIC HOME SEEN ON THE OPENING CREDITS OF THE POPULAR TV SHOW FULL HOUSE.

Architect: Charles Hinkel Lewis

"Full House" 1892-1896 San Francisco, California

ARTS & CRAFTS 1860-1920

STARTED IN ENGLAND THEN CAME TO AMERICA

REJECTION OF CHEAP AND OVER-MACHINED ELEMENTS FROM INDUSTRIAL REVOLUTION

&

REACTION TO THE ORNAMENTATION OF VICTORIAN ERA APPRECIATING SIMPLICITY

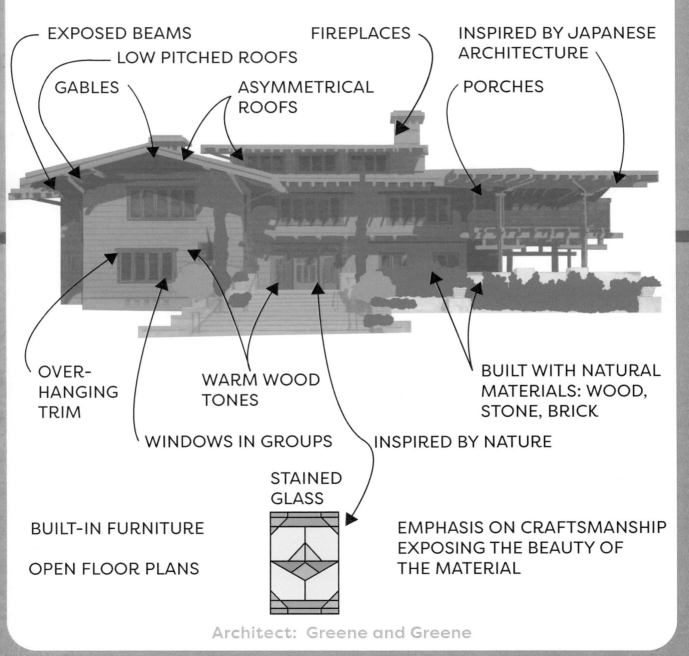

EXPOSED BEAMS

LOW PITCHED ROOFS

GABLES

ASYMMETRICAL ROOFS

FIREPLACES

INSPIRED BY JAPANESE ARCHITECTURE

PORCHES

OVER-HANGING TRIM

WARM WOOD TONES

WINDOWS IN GROUPS

INSPIRED BY NATURE

STAINED GLASS

BUILT WITH NATURAL MATERIALS: WOOD, STONE, BRICK

BUILT-IN FURNITURE

OPEN FLOOR PLANS

EMPHASIS ON CRAFTSMANSHIP EXPOSING THE BEAUTY OF THE MATERIAL

Architect: Greene and Greene

Gamble House, 1908 Pasadena, California

ART NOUVEAU 1890-1910

FUNDAMENTAL NEW APPROACH TO ARCHITECTURE. BREAK AWAY FROM HISTORICAL STYLES. ART NOUVEAU MEANS "NEW STYLE".

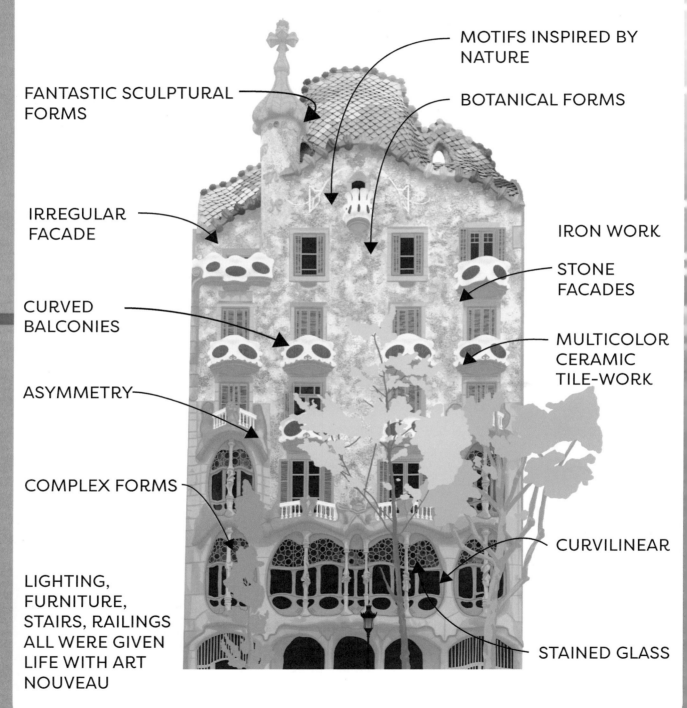

MOTIFS INSPIRED BY NATURE

FANTASTIC SCULPTURAL FORMS

BOTANICAL FORMS

IRREGULAR FACADE

IRON WORK

STONE FACADES

CURVED BALCONIES

MULTICOLOR CERAMIC TILE-WORK

ASYMMETRY

COMPLEX FORMS

CURVILINEAR

LIGHTING, FURNITURE, STAIRS, RAILINGS ALL WERE GIVEN LIFE WITH ART NOUVEAU

STAINED GLASS

Architect: Antoni Gaudi

Casa Batllo 1904-1912 Barcelona, Spain

INTERNATIONAL 1920-1940

VILLA SAVOYE IS AN EXAMPLE OF LE CORBUSIER'S 1927 PRINCIPLE OF THE FIVE POINTS OF ARCHITECTURE A FUNDAMENTAL PRINCIPLE IN THE INTERNATIONAL AND MODERN MOVEMENT

POINT #5 FLAT ROOFS:
ALLOWS FOR GARDEN ON TOP. IF YOU BUILD ON GREEN-SPACE YOU SHOULD REPLACE WHAT YOU TOOK AWAY.

POINT #4 WINDOWS:
HORIZONTAL WINDOWS ALLOWING MORE LIGHT TO ENTER.

LACK OF DECORATION

FLAT SURFACES

USE OF CONCRETE, STONE AND GLASS

BOXLIKE STRUCTURES

POINT #1 PILOTIS:
REINFORCED CONCRETE COLUMNS IN A GRID ON GROUND LEVEL MUST BE LOAD BEARING

POINT #2 FREE DESIGN:
PILOTIS REPLACE THE NEED OF LOAD BEARING WALLS ALLOWING FOR OPEN FLOOR PLANS AND FREEDOM WITH DESIGN FOR SPACE PLANNING.

POINT #3 FACADE:
THE EXTERIOR OF THE BUILDING CAN HAVE FREEDOM WITH DESIGN SINCE IT IS NOT LOAD BEARING

ARCHITECT LE CORBUSIER WAS KNOWN TO HAVE A MORE FEMINIST ATTITUDE. HE HIRED FEMALE ARCHITECTS AND HAD THEM WORKING SIDE BY SIDE WITH MEN.

Architect: Le Corbusier

Villa Savoye 1931 Poissy, France

ART DECO 1925-1937

ART DECO FIRST EVOLVED IN FRANCE. A FASHION INSPIRED DESIGN, ART DECO FOUND INSPIRATION IN ART, JAZZ AND DECORATION.

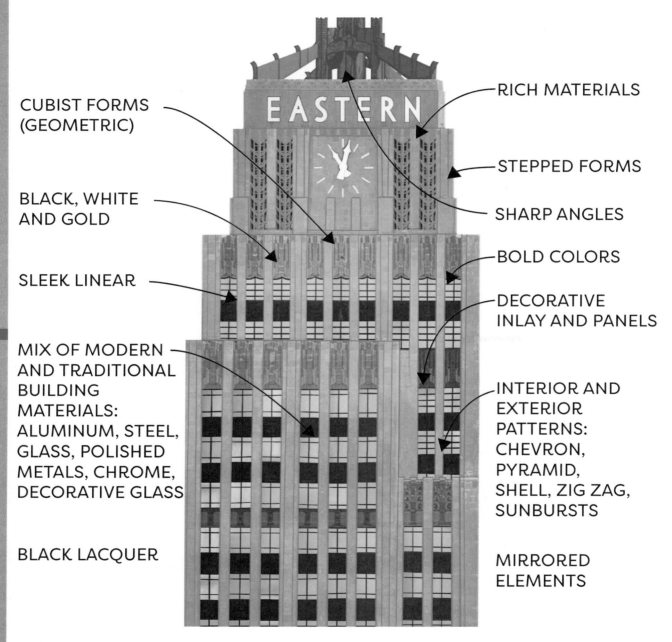

CUBIST FORMS (GEOMETRIC)

BLACK, WHITE AND GOLD

SLEEK LINEAR

MIX OF MODERN AND TRADITIONAL BUILDING MATERIALS: ALUMINUM, STEEL, GLASS, POLISHED METALS, CHROME, DECORATIVE GLASS

BLACK LACQUER

RICH MATERIALS

STEPPED FORMS

SHARP ANGLES

BOLD COLORS

DECORATIVE INLAY AND PANELS

INTERIOR AND EXTERIOR PATTERNS: CHEVRON, PYRAMID, SHELL, ZIG ZAG, SUNBURSTS

MIRRORED ELEMENTS

ART DECO ARCHITECTURE WAS PRIMARILY SEEN IN COMMERCIAL BUILDINGS AND LESS IN RESIDENTIAL HOMES. HOWEVER ART DECO LIGHTING FIXTURES, ARTWORK, FURNITURE AND TEXTILES WERE SEEN IN MANY DIFFERENT INTERIOR SPACES.

Architect: Claud Beelman

Eastern Columbia Building 1930 Los Angeles, California

MID CENTURY MODERNISM 1933-1965

POWER DESIGN COUPLE CHARLES AND RAY EAMES DESIGNED THEIR HOME TOGETHER. THE HOUSE WAS KNOWN AS "CASE STUDY HOUSE NUMBER 8" A PROGRAM THAT CHALLENGED ARCHITECTS TO DESIGN MODERN AND INEXPENSIVE HOMES IN POSTWAR SOUTHERN CALIFORNIA.

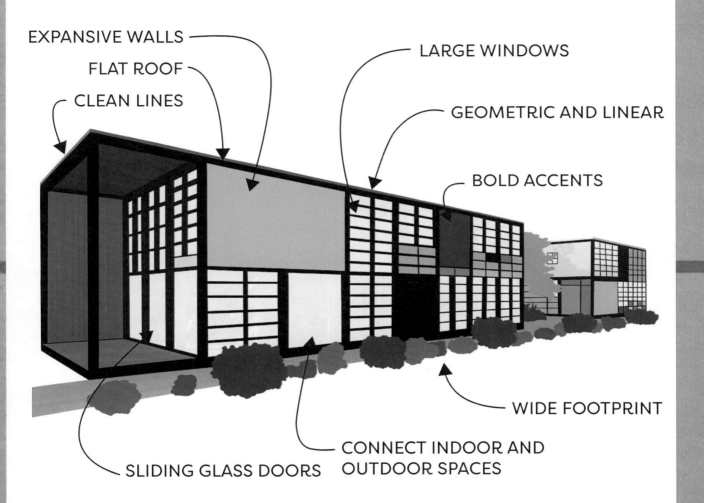

EXPANSIVE WALLS

FLAT ROOF

CLEAN LINES

LARGE WINDOWS

GEOMETRIC AND LINEAR

BOLD ACCENTS

WIDE FOOTPRINT

SLIDING GLASS DOORS

CONNECT INDOOR AND OUTDOOR SPACES

INTERIOR DESIGN FOCUSED ON FUNCTIONALITY

AFTER WORLD WAR II AMERICANS FOCUSED ON FAMILY CONNECTIONS AND LIFESTYLE INCORPORATING OPEN FLOOR PLANS FOR THE WHOLE FAMILY TO GATHER TOGETHER.

Architect: Charles and Ray Eames

Eames House 1949 Pacific Palisades, California

MODERNISM 1930-PRESENT

MODERN ARCHITECTURE HAS TAKEN DIFFERENT SHAPES OVER TIME. IT IS A TIME WHEN HISTORICAL STYLES WERE SET ASIDE. EXPERIMENTATION AND A BREAK FROM TRADITION TOOK PLACE.

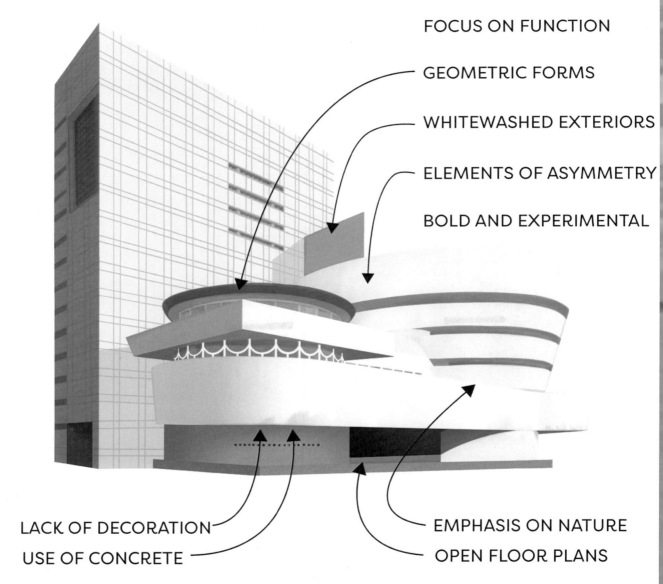

FOCUS ON FUNCTION

GEOMETRIC FORMS

WHITEWASHED EXTERIORS

ELEMENTS OF ASYMMETRY

BOLD AND EXPERIMENTAL

LACK OF DECORATION

USE OF CONCRETE

EMPHASIS ON NATURE

OPEN FLOOR PLANS

ORGANIC ARCHITECTURE: FRANK LLOYD WRIGHT'S PHILOSOPHY WAS THAT BUILDINGS SHOULD DEVELOP FROM THEIR SURROUNDINGS AND THE FUNCTION OF THE BUILDING. THE INTERIOR OF THE MUSEUM IS A LONG CONTINUOUS RAMP DESCENDING THROUGH THE SPIRAL ENCOURAGING REFLECTION AND APPRECIATION OF THE ART ON DISPLAY.

Architect: Frank Lloyd Wright

Solomon R. Guggenheim Museum 1959 New York, New York

BRUTALISM 1950-1980

BRUTALISM COMES FROM THE FRENCH TERM "BÉTON BRUT" MEANING "RAW CONCRETE"

MOST OFTEN USED FOR INSTITUTIONAL BUILDINGS

LOTS OF TEXTURE

STRENGTH IN STRUCTURE

MODULAR ELEMENTS

SMALL WINDOWS

EMPHASIS ON MATERIALS

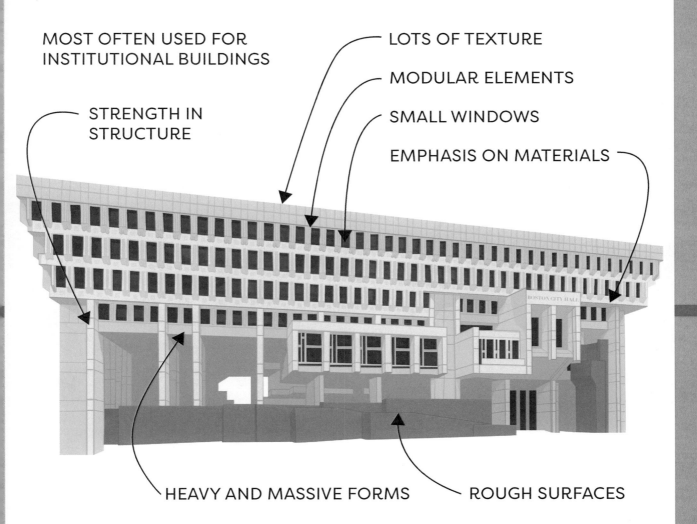

HEAVY AND MASSIVE FORMS

ROUGH SURFACES

AFTER ITS UPRISE BRUTALISM BECAME LABELED AS ARCHITECTURE WITH BAD TASTE; IT WAS DESCRIBED AS COLD AND UNWELCOMING.

BOSTON CITY HALL WAS INTENTED TO SHOW THE CONNECTION BETWEEN THE CITY GOVERNMENT AND ITS COMMUNITY. FLOORS WERE DIVIDED BY FUNCTION LEAVING THE LOWER ACCESSIBLE LEVELS OPEN TO THE PUBLIC.

Architect: Kallmann McKinnell & Wood

Boston City Hall 1963-1969 Boston, Massachusetts

POST MODERNISM 1960-2000

POSTMODERN ARCHITECTURE WAS A REACTION TO THE WHITEWASHED, PLAIN MODERN ARCHITECTURE. IT BROUGHT BACK CLASSICAL ARCHITECTURAL ELEMENTS FROM THE PAST, BUT PUT A SPIN ON THEM.

EYE CATCHING

LIVELY COLORS

WHIMSICAL

EXAGGERATED FORMS

ANIMAL SHAPED PEDIMENTS

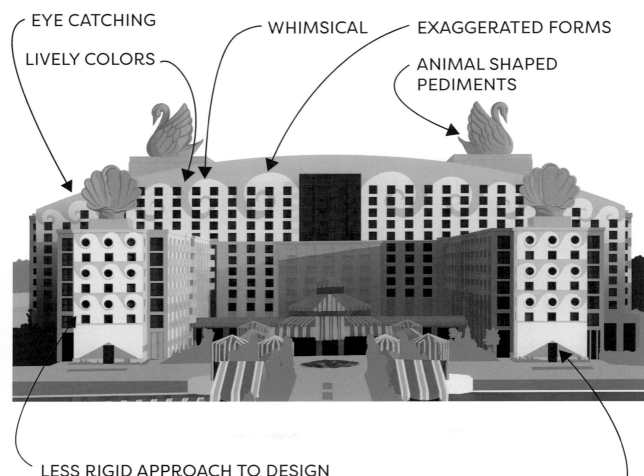

LESS RIGID APPROACH TO DESIGN

EXPERIMENT WITH CLASSICAL AND HISTORICAL ELEMENTS

OFTEN CHARATERIZED BY A LACK OF FUNCTION, PARTICULARLY WITH FURNITURE.

Architect: Michael Graves

The Swan Hotel Walt Disney World 1990 Orlando, Florida

DECONSTRUCTIVISM 1988-PRESENT

THE ABILITY TO MANIPULATE ARCHITECTURE THROUGH COMPUTER DESIGN ALLOWED FOR MORE 3D DIGITAL MODELING, PARAMETRIC DESIGN AND NEW APPLICATION OF MATERIALS. IT INFLUENCED PUBLIC ARCHITECTURE: MUSEUMS, CONCERT HALLS, PERFORMING ARTS CENTERS, TRANSPORTATION FACILITIES, LIBRARIES, RELIGIOUS STRUCTURES AND MORE.

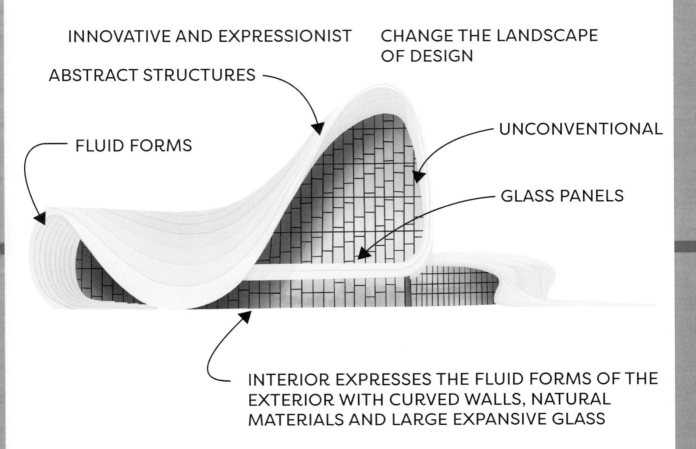

INNOVATIVE AND EXPRESSIONIST

CHANGE THE LANDSCAPE OF DESIGN

ABSTRACT STRUCTURES

UNCONVENTIONAL

FLUID FORMS

GLASS PANELS

INTERIOR EXPRESSES THE FLUID FORMS OF THE EXTERIOR WITH CURVED WALLS, NATURAL MATERIALS AND LARGE EXPANSIVE GLASS

BIOMORPHISM: ARCHITECTURE BASED ON HUMAN AND ANIMAL FORMS INSPIRED BY NATURE; UNDULATING STRUCTURES, FLEXIBLE MATERIALS AND FREE-FORM COMPUTER AIDED DESIGN.

ZAHA HADID DESIGNED THIS CULTURAL CENTER AS A DEPARTURE FROM RIGID SOVIET ARCHITECTURE IN BAKU, TO EXPRESS THE VALUES OF THE AZERBAIJAN CULTURE OF OPTIMISM AND EXCITEMENT FOR THE FUTURE.

Architect: Zaha Hadid

Heydar Aliyev Center 2012 Baku, Azerbaijan

· GIVE WOMEN A VOICE IN ARCHITECTURE ·

PRITZKER PRIZE PETITION

SEATTLE ART MUSEUM · SAINSBURY WING · AIA GOLD METAL · UNIVERSITY OF PENNSYLVANIA · JANE DREW PRIZE BEN FRANKLIN MEDAL · ROBERT VENTURI · ASSOCIATION SCHOOL OF ARCHITECTURE · ALLEN MEMORIAL ART MUSEUM · LEARNING FROM LAS VEGAS THE VIEW FROM THE CAMPIDOGLIO CONCEPTS · NATIONAL MUSEUM & SCHOOL ACADEMY OF ARTS AN AMERICAN PHILOSO AMERICAN PLAN ARCHITECTS

PLANNERSFOR ATHENAEUM OF THE ARCHITECT LONDON · CARP OF THE CITY A PHILADELPHIA · RO OF THE BRITISH INTERNATIONAL FELLOW · GOLD MEDAL · ROYAL SOCIETY FOR THE ARTS, MANUFACTURE & COMMERC SOCIETY OF COLLEGE & UNIVERS PLANNING · MEDAL OF HONOR, BUND DEUTSCHER ARCHI WITWATERSRAND LIFETIME ACHI

ROYAL SOCIETY FOR THE ARTS MANUFACTURE & COMMERCE SOCIETY OF COLLEGE & UNIVERSIT PLANNING · MEDAL OF HONOR, NYC BUND DEUTSCHER ARCHITEKTEI JANE DREW PRIZE· ARCHITIZER'S A+ LIFETIME ACHIEVEMEN AWARD GOLD MEDAL AMERICAI OF ARCHITECTS SOPHICAL SOCIET CIATIOI AND NSIBILIT PHIA JR NIA BER OLO A G FROM OM THE CONCEPTS MY MUSEUM AN ACADEMY CIENCES AL SOCIET OCIATION AND

Denise Scott Brown 1931

Denise was born in 1931 in Northern Rhodesia, in Africa. She was raised by her Jewish parents Simon and Phyllis Lakofski. Denise began her studies at a university in South Africa, where she met her future husband, Robert Scott Brown. From there the pair moved to London where Denise studied at the Architectural Association School, earning her architecture degree in 1955 and getting married that same year. At the age of 27, Denise left for the United States and landed in Philadelphia with her husband by her side. After four short years of marriage, Robert was tragically killed in a car accident. Determined, Denise pushed herself forward, earning another degree, a Master's Degree in City Planning and Architecture from the University of Pennsylvania (UPenn). Denise met her second husband, architect Robert Venturi, at the university. The pair taught courses together at UPenn for a few years as they built their relationship. Denise's commitment to academia led her to teach at many other schools, including Harvard, UCLA, UC Berkeley, and Yale. Her research and publications have influenced and inspired designers and students all over the world.

After Denise married Robert in 1967, together they started the design firm Venturi, Scott Brown and Associates (VSBA). Denise led the urban planning, design and campus planning projects. Denise and Robert together are credited with defining the postmodern movement in architecture. The earliest example is the extension to the Allen Memorial Art Museum in Ohio, designed in 1976. VSBA prides itself on collaboration and team building, but the media and the architecture field took this from them. Denise was excluded from the press and the accolades that their projects earned. She was often considered the "wife" of the architect and was not invited or welcomed to the meetings. Denise documented these inequalities in her 1989 essay "Room at the Top? Sexism and the Star System in Architecture." Just three short years after this publication, she received the largest blow. In 1991, the Pritzker Prize, one of the greatest recognitions in the field of design, was awarded solely to her husband Robert Venturi. This was denying the pair's beliefs and statements about how they saw themselves as equal partners. Denise did not attend the awards ceremony as her protest against the injustice.

Denise continued to impact the landscape of architecture through her works, writings and teaching. A petition was made in her honor to stand up against the discrimination, gaining over 20,000 signatures. Denise has been recognized for over 40 awards, written over 150 publications, and in 2017 won the Jane Drew Prize for Women in Architecture. Her groundbreaking strength and conviction in the face of discrimination in the field of architecture is heroic.

of urban design, her firm produced in 1997 a model for ma
proposed changes to zoning laws to accommodate this

Max novative project was her renovation
ulate Heart of Mary sisterhood (2
blicized as an ecologically
of the sisterho
ectural Institute
ca Méxicana (she holds honorary
win graduat 93) and the versity of Detroit Mercy
the Mayor ommendation from the C Phila enre
s, ished Daught of ylvania 1995), and
xman f nced six Ceiling Award y t

professor classes. Stanislaw
d number

g Maxma
Nowick ite excited
women
more ir
As sign" in
or Sportso thesis
ch it and ped in reading a
comp f university of Pe
g Aut rpo odFine
mmuni a mod
magazin

career, her design s, and joint d nty for Girl Scouts ovate credentia
v projects, prototyp as a campi the AIA Honor Award he
cts, Camp Tweed le an Archit ntral assembly hall,
hich French doors allow

only three years
sylvania. Therm quick
a client base thro
of a space
Together Sutple
knowledged that her

Susan Maxman   1938

One hundred and thirty-five years after its inception, the American Institute of Architects (AIA) elected their first national female president, and that was Susan Maxman. Susan was born in Columbus, Ohio, one of three girls in her family. When Susan grew up, it was assumed that women would be stay-at-home moms attending social events and offering their free time to charity work. At a young age, Susan knew this would not be her path. Without many role models leading the way, she set off to pursue her dream of becoming an architect.

Susan started her college career at Smith College in Northampton, Massachusetts. Being surrounded by intelligent, capable and passionate women was inspiring to her. At the young age of 20, Susan married and followed her husband to the University of Pennsylvania. She planned to enter the undergraduate program in architecture but was told that women were not welcome. Bewildered and disappointed, she decided to pursue a degree in art history. The pregnancy and the birth of her first child put all of that on hold. Child rearing often slowed or stopped a woman's advancement in her career or schooling at that time, as it was often expected that she would stay home or that the time away would slow a womans progression in education or her career. Susan's first marriage did not last and in 1971 she married William Maxman. With six kids all together, three from each partner's previous marriage, their family buzzed with energy.

Susan is a life long learner. In 1972 she returned to the University of Pennsylvania at age 30. At this time the number of women studying architecture was climbing. Frustrated after graduation by the unequal pay between men and women in the field of architecture, she started her own architecture firm with a classmate. Susan pushed forward in a male-dominated and sometimes unwelcoming working world. She became involved in local organizations and took on more and more responsibilities in her community, all the while creating a well-known and respected architecture firm. Susan also took an interest in sustainable design and developed projects with an ecological conscience. In 1992 Susan became the first female president of the AIA! Being in the spotlight allowed Susan to share her eco-friendly design thinking with a larger audience. She was involved with the 1992 Earth Summit and she also planned the AIA convention in Chicago. The conference focused on the future of the built environment and architecture as it relates to climate change. Susan took her groundbreaking role as president and used it to raise awareness and be the role model for women. She is recognized for her groundbreaking efforts in architecture, leadership, and advocacy for equality.

Clodagh

Born in a tiny town near the west coast of Ireland, Clodagh took the road less traveled. At age 15 Clodagh suffered a horse-riding accident that broke her back and landed her in the hospital for a long year of recovery. While she was bedridden she was an avid reader of books, magazines and current events. Her mom often brought her the Irish Times to read. On one particular occasion she read an article that changed the course of her life. The article was about being a fashion designer, posing the question "Why not?" This became her motto moving forward throughout her life and career.

Shortly after getting out of the hospital, Clodagh had just turned 17. She dropped her last name and took off to Dublin to open a fashion house. Setting aside her father's goal of her becoming a professor, she was determined to make a life of her own persuasion. She developed a recognized fashion style in Dublin, growing her business over the years. She married and had three sons during her time as a fashionista.

Eventually she married for the second time and moved to Spain. There she uncovered her passion for design. While remodeling a home, she found herself re-working the architect's drawings. Her eye for design began to flourish and she started working in architecture, interiors and furniture design. In 1983 Clodagh and her husband Daniel Aubry moved to New York City. Daniel had set his sights on the land where dreams are made. Reluctant at first, Clodagh joined him for the journey and in 1989 she founded Clodagh Design.

Clodagh has evolved design to focus on the well-being of the user. She was one of the first designers to explore and implement Feng Shui, the study of orientation, placement and arrangement that can harmonize a space. Driven by the understanding that our environment can affect our mental health and that space can be a sensory experience, Clodagh broke ground on holistic design thinking. It is not just about the finished product, it is the journey of the design process and ensuring clients and their needs are brought to the forefront. She incorporates chromotherapy (using color as a healing method), biophilia (using natural elements or elements inspired by nature to benefit well-being), and sustainability in her design methods. Her "life-enhancing minimalism" is the foundation of her practice. Spaces can impact our lives and she does it with out clutter and chaos. She believes in the idea that thoughtful design can improve our well-being. Clodagh is on a journey to create spaces that bring people peace and serenity to comfort their mind, body and soul.

GREEN architecture
green buildings

water conservation collected, stored, filtered, and reused, low flow plumbing fixtures

indoor environmental quality lighting, air quality. wellness for people in the building

energy efficiency use less energy to heat, cool and run appliances. create your own energy

materials and resources use eco-friendly materials made from renewable resources and recyclable

site and community impact respect natural surroundings, reduce negative effects on community

adaptive reuse re-purposing of an existing structure for new use
historic preservation preserve old or historic buildings

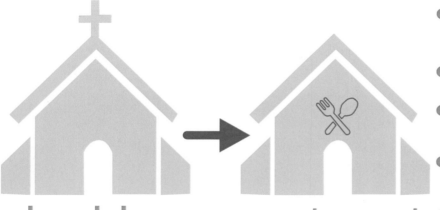

church becomes restaurant

- adapts to current and future needs
- reduces waste
- preserves architectural character
- pushes innovation and creativity
- saves money

use fewer resources, improve human and environmental health and happiness

biophillia

human beings instinct to connect with nature

benefits of connecting to nature in our built environment (home, work, school)

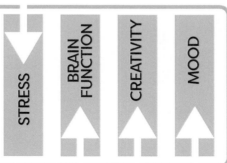

STRESS · BRAIN FUNCTION · CREATIVITY · MOOD

defined by Dr. Edward O. Wilson in 1973 natural environments are critical to our health and wellness incorporate natural shapes, forms and elements in design

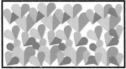

green wall/ live wall

water element

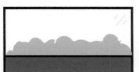

plants and daylight

natural materials

green roof

mimicking patterns in nature

sustainability

focused on the future

environment

reduce our impact on the planet and natural resources

renewable resources
recycled products
reduce air pollution
energy conservation

economy

economic growth

more green jobs

energy savings

cost saving on operating a building

rebuilding communities

society

Buildings provide: occupant comfort

daylight, connection to nature

People benefit: well-being, healthy resources, provide for future generations

"YOU MUST BELIEVE IN YOURSELF, IN YOUR PASSION, YOUR CREATIVITY AND YOUR ABILITY"

Yasmeen Lari   1941

Yasmeen Lari is Pakistan's first woman architect. In a culture where women do not have equal rights or receive the same treatment as men, and where women suffer violence and injustice, Yasmeen persevered. She grew up admiring her father's work as an architect. He was involved in large-scale urban planning projects, all of which inspired Yasmeen to pursue the same path. At age 15 she left Pakistan for London England. There she studied art and in 1964 she graduated from the Oxford School of Architecture. With her father's concern about the lack of qualified architects in Pakistan, Yasmeen moved back with her husband to open their own practice, Lari Associates.

Yasmeen was a pioneer of brutalist architecture in Pakistan, designing homes and buildings, often made of concrete, with a rigid, geometric and monolithic or monstrous style. Over the next 30 years, her firm was involved in large corporate and hospitality projects. While she was part of these large-scale elite projects, she was also committed to developing social housing, homes that are affordable for poor people within her community. In 1980 Yasmeen and her husband started the Heritage Foundation of Pakistan, dedicated to documenting and conserving traditional and historic buildings and promoting Pakistan's architectural history and cultural heritage.

In the year 2000, Yasmeen retired from her firm to pursue a national advisor role with the United Nations Educational, Scientific and Cultural Organization (UNESCO), an international collaboration on human rights. She also wanted to focus more of her time on her foundation. Five years into her retirement, Yasmeen's calling took a turn. Pakistan suffered a devastating 7.8-magnitude earthquake that killed 80,000 people and displaced 400,000 families. Yasmeen dedicated her work to teaching locals how to build low-cost, zero-carbon, eco-friendly homes and community centers that can withstand natural disasters, a process for which she coined the term "Barefoot Social Architecture." She helped to create 40,000 homes that have withstood floods and earthquakes. In a community where there are high levels of poverty, Yasmeen is working to give these marginalized often forgotten groups the tools to take charge of their own lives, teaching them ways to strengthen the sustainability of their community and the environment. In 2020 Yasmeen earned the Jane Drew Prize —an award recognizing a person for their efforts within innovation, inclusion and diversity—for raising the profile of women in architecture, which in turn raised the profile of women in Pakistan.

Sunita Kohli   1946

Born in Lahore, Pakistan near the border of India, Sunita has always been interested in history. During her childhood she explored auctions and antique shops with her father. She studied English literature in college, earning both a bachelor's and a master's degree in the subject. In 1971, at age 25, Sunita founded her own firm focused on sourcing authentic antique furniture from the 1800s.

Over time her interest in furniture and design opened the doors to interior design projects. With her passion and interest in history, design, research and restoration, Sunita became a very successful self-taught interior designer. Sunita completed a range of projects, from residences to large-scale public and heritage buildings, hotels, palaces, libraries and more.

Sunita quickly became a leader in architectural restoration and historic preservation. On projects she spent hours studying the original architect's design intentions to maintain the true objective of the space. While creating impressive interiors, Sunita manufactured contemporary and classical furniture pieces of her own. Her trailblazing accomplishments did not go unnoticed. In 1991, Mother Teresa awarded Sunita the Mahila Shiromani award, recognizing her as a woman of achievement. Most notable in 1992, Sunita was awarded the prestigious "Padma Shri" award from the president of India, the highest national award. This recognized Sunita's contributions in architectural restoration and design, and was the first time in history this award was given to an interior designer.

Sunita became a sought-after lecturer, speaking to students all over the world. Her words inspired others and her mission was incredibly important. In 2005 Sunita founded the Museum of Women in Arts in India, to share the incredible skill and achievements of women artists inspiring the next generation. As her mission grew and the demands for her skills and knowledge multiplied, Sunita was joined in New Delhi by her daughter Kohelika, an American-trained architect. They merged in 2010 to start their firm K2 India, combining all their skills under one roof. Four years later Sunita was elected the chairperson of the School of Planning and Architecture in Bhopal, a National Institute of Excellence. Sunita was the first woman ever appointed to this position; there she was asked to define and implement a new vision for architecture in India. Sunita's respect for the past and dedication to restoring, sharing, and preserving it has truly landed her a place in the world of interior design. Design is not only about creating something new, it is also about appreciating what has been created before us. Sunita is a pioneer in her field, open to the future while respecting the past.

Zaha Hadid

Bending buildings to do the unimaginable. Zaha Hadid has left her futuristic mark on the global architectural landscape. Born in 1950 in Iraq, Zaha had always loved numbers. Her favorite subject in school was math. Zaha was born into a wealthy progressive family who welcomed her role as a strong female. When she began her undergraduate studies, she studied math at the American University of Beirut. In 1972 she moved to London to pursue her master's degree in architecture. A risk-taker at heart, Zaha challenged architecture and the role of women in architecture. She showed up strong, determined and confident.

Zaha's architectural style was futuristic and inventive. She made concrete, steel and glass look alive, taking on unexplained shapes that were soft and fluid. She would amaze people with her architectural creations and then astound them with another unexpected design. Zaha often designed buildings for the public, with many of her creations able to be experienced by people from all different walks of life. She mystified and enlightened the museum experience with rolling concrete and sharp angles. Along with museums, she also designed an opera house, cultural centers, pavilions and even the aquatic center in London that was used for the 2021 Summer Olympics.

Alongside her daring architecture she was a woman of many firsts. In 2004 she changed the landscape of recognition for female architects; 40 years after the first Pritzker Prize was awarded, Zaha was the first woman to win the most sought-after award in architecture. In 2016, after 168 years of male dominance, the Royal Gold Medal was awarded to Zaha.

While her projects were dynamic and jaw dropping, she continued to be confronted throughout her career because of her gender and nationality. She often felt like she was not accepted, but she refused to ask for permission or approval and pushed forward. Zaha was unconventional and people felt as though they had the right to criticize her.

Zaha's career was cut short at the young age of 65 when she died of a heart attack. It is no surprise that in her lifetime Zaha was named one of the "World's Most Powerful Women." She laid the foundation for other women to feel empowered to step up and make a name for themselves in the field of architecture. While she rarely engaged in the conversation of gender in the field of architecture she knew she inspired women and she was happy with that. She convinced others to take risks, experiment, and dream beyond the imaginable.

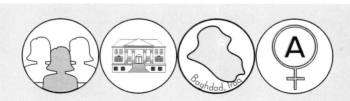

first woman to
design a mosque

Zeynep Fadıllıoğlu   1955

Raised in a grand waterfront mansion on the shores of the Bosphorus Strait in Istanbul, Turkey, Zeynep was surrounded by opulence and rich architectural history. She was already collecting art at the age of 14, with the guidance of her father. Both of her grandfathers were in the textile business, inspiring her passion for fabrics and antiques. With encouragement from her father, Zeynep moved to London and studied art history at the Inchbald School of Design.

Zeynep returned to Turkey and married Metin Fadıllıoğlu, a well-known restaurateur. As her husband opened some of the most successful establishments in Istanbul, she was by his side working as the interior designer of his restaurants. This launched her into pursuing the career of architecture and interior design. In 1995 she opened her own design firm, where she surrounded herself with a strong interdisciplinary team bringing together all different professionals in the field. While she was not formally educated in architecture or design, she certainly has a vision and she leans on her team to help make her designs a reality. Her art background inspires her design, combining Eastern and Western styles as well as blending contemporary and traditional architecture. Zeynep pushes boundaries with her bold style, telling stories of the past and articulating them through pattern, texture and color.

While her projects were noteworthy and beautiful, it was in 2009 that Zeynep won the commission to design the Şakirin Mosque in Istanbul. She is regarded as the first woman to ever design a mosque. This achievement goes well beyond the architecture and design, as it challenges the role of women in Turkey, a culture where female independence is threatened and the gender divide is tangible. She did not evade criticism and doubt as she drove her design forward. Zeynep transformed the mosque with an exquisite blend of modern and antique design references. She used pattern and texture as ways to transform light. She used color to create focus and transition. Zeynep's design celebrates the Muslim culture while refreshing traditional values. Men and women are expected to worship separately in a mosque. Men remain on the main floor and women are ushered off to another location, typically an uninspiring smaller space, often in the back. Zeynep designed the women's worship gallery to be beautiful and open. There women can worship comfortably and feel significant.

Zeynep is a true example of how design can not only transform our experience but can also be progressive and make a meaningful difference to the users of the space. In her mosque design, she made the women feel special and important as they worshiped. She worked to bring equity in experience through design.

INCLUSIVE DESIGN
observation + research +

culture   mental health   age   neurological disorders   race   gender

Americans with Disability Act protection from discrimination

Universal Design designing for all

Human Factors interaction of individuals with their environment

Anthropometrics scientific study of the measurements of a human

Aging in Place the ability to live in your home safely as you age

Cultural Awareness being conscious of other cultures and their values

Physical Needs things that are necessary to survive

Emotional Needs our range of feelings; sad, happy, scared, excited...

Physiological Needs biological needs, what our body needs to function

= design for everyone
creativity + problem solving

visual impairment   hearing impairment   neurodevelopmental disorders

USER FOCUSED

listen to peoples' needs

Research
Recognize
Respect
differences

healthcare design

focus on wellbeing

users: patients, staff, families, caregivers

design for all age groups and abilities

create a healing environment

education design

no student left behind

design for all learning modalities and styles

public design

| design for all |
| same opportunity for all users |
| clear way-finding |
| safety for all users |

ramps benefit wheelchair users, strollers, travelers with suitcases and elderly

 flexible seating options in a classroom allow students to have a choice and serve their needs

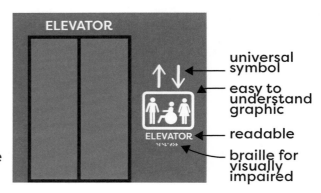

ELEVATOR

universal symbol

easy to understand graphic

readable

braille for visually impaired

ELEVATOR

Americans with Disability Act (ADA)

signed into law in 1990

prohibits discrimination against people with disabilities

In 2010 regulations were revised and became enforceable accessibility standards called the 2010 ADA Standards for Accessible Design

Guidelines and Standards establish design requirements for:

public spaces
commercial facilities
state and local
government buildings

new construction
alterations
additions

bathrooms,
hallways, stairs,
doorways,
ramps, signage
way-finding,
built-ins,
amusement
rides

*and much more

UNIVERSAL DESIGN

designing for all people regardless of their ability

7 PRINCIPLES

1. Equitable Use
same experience for all users

2. Flexible in Use
flexible and adaptable design

3. Simple and Intuitive Use
use of design is easy to understand

4. Perceptible Information
information is easy to access

5. Tolerance for Error
safe and reduce hazards

6. Low Physical Effort
design can be used with ease

7. Size and Space for Approach and Use
space works for all sizes and mobility

multiple seating options at the window with a view

powered desk with height options

color contrast to help designate space

use pictures along with words

decals on a glass door

automatic light sensors

ample circulation space

ergonomics

WHAT scientific understanding of how humans interact with their environment

GOAL increase efficiency, productivity and reduce discomfort

HOW

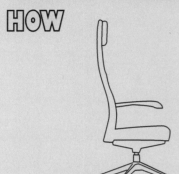

chairs that are better for our posture

adjustable lighting

anthropometrics

WHAT the study of measuring size and proportion of the human body

GOAL to make everyone as comfortable as possible

HOW

ceiling heights

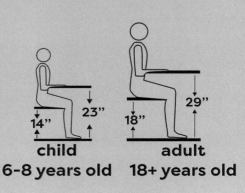

14"   23"

child
6-8 years old

18"   29"

adult
18+ years old

aging in place

WHAT adults who want to remain in their home as they age

GOAL plan ahead and design for the needs as the user ages

HOW

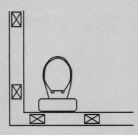

put structure in walls in case you need to add grab bars someday, this reduces waste during remodeling and saves time and money

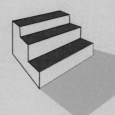

contrasting colors to help define depth as vision fades

cultural awareness

WHAT being aware of other cultures and how they will interact with the environment

GOAL research and be inclusive of other cultures' needs, traditions and values. Design responsibly.

HOW

don't design with sacred objects without understanding meaning

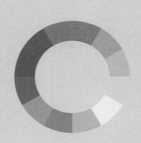

understand the meaning of colors to other cultures

Odile Decq

A raven of an architect, Odile Decq is known for her all-black, Gothic style and her radical architecture. Born in a small town in France, Odile did not see a female architect until she left for university. On the tails of her graduation, she started her own firm and began entering design competitions to get her name out in the field. She fought off the backlash she received not only as a woman in the field but also because of her unconventional appearance. Early on, she realized that those who judged her based on her looks and did not give her a chance were not worth her time.

Odile found a partner in business and in life. She married Benoît Cornette, who was her champion and she was his. He joined her firm and they designed under the joint name ODBC Architects. They shook up the French landscape with daring and dynamic designs. In 1998, Odile suffered the great loss of her husband in a car accident. Not until 15 years later did she change the name of her firm; up until that point she attributed all her great designs to them both.

Her portfolio is full of risk-taking and rebellion. She has designed public spaces, apartment buildings, office buildings, and furniture, and crafted the urban landscape. Odile blends the urban landscape into her designs, embracing and challenging the site in unexpected and innovative ways. In many of her designs you will see her signature pop of red, bringing her courage and energy into her environments as a focal point. Beyond her architecture, Odile is committed to the future of architecture and architects.

Odile returned to her university, Ecole Speciale d'Architecure, to teach and in 2007 was elected as a dean. Odile challenged their traditional ways and received a mix of criticism and support. Determined to change the way architecture was taught, Odile launched her own architectural school. The Confluence Institute for Innovation and Creative Strategies is a liberal multidisciplinary architectural college, bringing together many different programs and departments to broaden the scope of learning established in 2014.

In 2018 Odile and a group of female architects protested the discrimination against women in the industry. They encouraged people to join them during the Venice Architecture Biennale, the 16th International Architecture Exhibition held in Italy. Odile urged women to stand up against the harassment and asserted that women architects are not invisible; rather, they are a powerful and necessary asset to the field. An advocate for women, education, individuality, Odile is tearing down the glass ceiling and welcoming women and younger generations to join her.

Karen Braitmayer

Karen has literally changed the landscape of architecture throughout her career. She grew up in the affluent town of Darien, Connecticut. Karen seemed a bit clumsy and was small for her age. Her parents noticed this but didn't think much of it. She didn't receive a diagnosis until she was six years old and she began using a wheelchair in elementary school in the 1960s. Karen was born with a genetic disorder called osteogenesis imperfecta which affects the strength of her bones. Karen's life in a wheelchair began before there were laws that required people to design accessible spaces. Karen was a true problem solver who would not take "no" for an answer. When she was told "no," she turned around and said, "let me try." Life in a wheelchair gave Karen a true perspective and a clear view into the challenges she faced in her community and the built environment.

After completing a degree in behavior sciences, Karen knew this was not the career for her. With a bit of research and identifying her interests, Karen set sail on the journey to getting her master's degree in Architecture from the University of Houston. Karen followed her passion to become an architect, even under the doubtful eyes of those around her. Whenever anyone said she could not do it, she proved them wrong and tried even harder. Karen has firsthand knowledge which continues to allow her to influence the design of the built environment. Karen's pursuit of an architecture degree is just as impactful as her career that followed.

Karen did not intend to be an advocate for accessibility; she wanted to be architect. It wasn't long before she could no longer stand to watch other people design inaccessible spaces and buildings. She found herself educating those around her about how their designs would not only affect her, but others in her community. It wasn't until 1990 that Congress passed the Americans with Disabilities Act, which required all new construction and renovation to provide accessible design. Inclusive design starts at the very beginning of any project. Understanding the users of the space is critical in every phase of design. In 1994 Karen opened her own consulting firm in Seattle, working with other architects on accessibility. It was her goal to inspire architects and designers to come up with creative and beautiful design solutions that met the building codes and the needs of the people.

In her career she has earned significant awards, appointments and honors, from the 2019 Mobility Person of the Year to the Whitney Young Award for Social Responsibility, as well as serving on the US Access Board. Most importantly, she has influenced architecture and design to accept a woman in a wheelchair as a leader, an inspiration, and an advocate for inclusivity in architecture and design.

Maya Lin 1959

A child of Chinese immigrants, Maya Lin grew up along with her brother in Athens, Ohio. Their parents fled China during the communist takeover and later met in the United States. Both of Maya's parents were professors at Ohio University. Education and academia played an integral role in the Lin Family.

Maya was a student at Yale University studying architecture when she had her very first groundbreaking moment as an architect. For a class project, she designed her version of the Vietnam Veterans Memorial. In 1982 while she was still at Yale, an opportunity arose to enter her design into a competition. Entries were judged blind, the judges didn't know anything about the people entering the competition, they didn't know their names, race, gender or anything else. Maya's design was selected out of over 1,400 applicants. Maya, a Chinese American female student won. Hiding the identities of the designers gave everyone an equal chance.

Her design literally broke ground, cutting into the landscape and creating a V-shaped path with walls of granite etched with the names of the 58,000 men and women who were killed or missing in action during the Vietnam War. She watched her design come to life among the inspiring monuments of Washington, DC. Unfortunately, her project was fraught with controversy, and, she was not named at its dedication. Today the memorial is one of the most-visited memorials in the nation's capital. Her goal was to honor the individuals lost and give a place for those left behind to feel grief, contemplate, and connect with the fallen soldiers, allowing visitors to see and touch their names.

After her first great accomplishment, Maya returned to academia and earned a Master's in Architecture from Yale University. In 1986 she founded her own studio. Her career since has continued to create public works that merge landscape, architecture and sculpture with an intense social impact. In 2009 she was awarded the National Medal of Arts and in 2016 the Presidential Medal of Freedom, both from President Barack Obama. Maya has completed works for the Civil Rights movement, including a memorial in Alabama. She has been involved in art installations and sculpture work. In 1993, the installation was completed of her sculpture <u>The Women's Table</u>, celebrating the inclusion of women at Yale University.

While students may not have completed their studies or earned their degree, they still have a voice. Opportunities are all around; a student should not be afraid to put themselves out there. As a student, Maya changed the landscape of architecture and inspired others around her. It is never too early to make a difference.

CHICAGO
USA

Jeanne Gang

An agent for change, architect Jeanne Gang was born and raised in the Midwest. As a young girl, Jeanne loved art and at one point thought about being an artist, but her love for math and science pushed her towards architecture, a beautiful mix of all three. Jeanne earned a bachelor's degree in Architecture from the University of Illinois in 1986. She went on to study urban design at the Institute of Technology in Zurich, Switzerland. From there she returned to the US to study earning her master's degree in Architecture at Harvard University. With her expansive knowledge and education, Jeanne landed back in Chicago. In 1997 Jeanne established her own firm, Studio Gang, an architecture and urbanism practice. Studio Gang has a powerful mission to activate communities, blending Jeanne's studies and passion for urban design and architecture. They refer to their process as "actionable idealism," the act of creating architecture that brings people together, connects users with nature, and respects and works in collaboration with the environment. Studio Gang is committed to the well-being of its users and our earth. These goals are evident in their portfolio of work.

Jeanne Gang led the design for the Aqua Tower, in 2010 it was the tallest woman-designed building in the world! The Aqua Tower is a true example of "Actionable Idealism". The facade or outside of the building resembles a topographical map with organic lines representing hills, valleys and water. The balconies vary allowing connections between the residents of the apartments. Inspired by the benefits of nature and social connections, the Aqua Tower is architectural artwork. But to Jeanne, the goal was not the accolades for height, it was the social and sustainable achievements of the building. In 2020 the St Regis Chicago building rose above the Aqua Tower becoming the tallest woman designed building in the world. Jeanne Gang was the mastermind behind that skyscraper as well!

Also an advocate for leveling the gender inequity playing field, Jeanne has led her firm to recognize and challenge the gender wage gap in the architecture field. She is an author, professor, and role model. In 2019 she was named one of the most influential people in the world by TIME magazine. Studio Gang goes beyond client-motivated projects and does extensive research on urban and architectural solutions for current issues and events. A topic of great concern is police violence and Studio Gang studied how design can connect police stations with the community to build relationships. Another example is a design for Chicago boathouses that filters storm water run-off organically to help the ecology of the river thrive.

Her projects are not only about the architecture, they engage with the users, the history, the environment, while collaborating with other disciplines, breaking barriers and mastering innovation.

Sheila Bridges

Born in Philadelphia, Pennsylvania, Sheila attended Brown University in Rhode Island and later earned a degree in interior design from Parsons School of Design in New York City. She also spent some time in Florence, Italy studying Italian art and architecture, which grew her passion for history. Sheila's design style is timeless and inspired. She has the ability to create a space that brings together different styles and colors in one harmonious, welcoming room. Sheila's interior design skills and attractive personality led her straight to stardom. She designed for celebrities, doctors and even former President Bill Clinton. She was featured in magazines and became a television personality.

As a black female interior designer, Sheila was making her mark on the design world. In 1993 she moved to New York City's Harlem neighborhood, where she was able to surround herself with the long history of African American culture. In 1994 Shelia started her own firm. With the inspiration of Harlem at her doorstep, Sheila's goal to offer culturally relevant and inspiring designs to her clients was her true motivation. She has earned many accolades, including America's Best Designer by TIME magazine and CNN in 2001. Her regular television appearances as an interior design expert, her publications, her furniture store in upstate New York, and her magazine features put Sheila in America's spotlight.

During the fourth season of her television show, Sheila began losing her hair. In her forties her appearance began to shift, leading to a period of healing and self-discovery. Her fans were worried she was sick and the television world was not ready to welcome a bald black woman. Sheila endured harsh comments about her appearance all while having to come to terms with her diagnosis of alopecia. After years of creating beautiful interiors, now she was challenged with her own beauty. After much hard work and reflection Sheila embraced her bald head, showing off her beauty and confidence.

Pushing forward with her career, Sheila introduced a fabric and wallpaper pattern, "Harlem Toile de Jouy." Looking through the historical toile patterns for projects, she could not find one that spoke to her heritage. Shelia updated this pattern, portraying scenes from African American urban and rural settings, sharing stereotypes of how black people were represented in that time.

Her courage, boldness and beauty are powerful. With her triumph over adversity, it is no wonder she was recently named on Architectural Digest's list of esteemed designers and architects from around the world.

Tamara Eagle Bull 1967

The first Native American female architect in the United States, she is a member of the Oglala Lakota Nation. Tamara Eagle Bull was raised in South Dakota. Tamara knew she had a knack for architecture at a young age. She could visualize three dimensionality and had a strong sense of space and design. Tamara's father, a schoolteacher, had once dreamed of being an architect. They would spend time talking about the good and bad of architecture and how it has affected the Native American community. With the help of the AIA Diversity Advancement Scholarship, Tamara was able to realize her dream of attending the University of Minnesota School of Architecture.

Shortly after graduation, she became an active member of the American Indian Council of Architects and Engineers. Much of Tamara's work is designing for Native American communities. Tamara is an advocate against cultural appropriation in architecture, looking for an end to the use of Native American symbols in design without understanding their meaning or context.

In 2018 Tamara Eagle Bull was awarded the Whitney Young award for preservation and respectful representation of Native American culture within tribal built environments. She is president of Encompass Architects, where 80% of their work is for Native American tribal communities. Some of her work includes community centers, schools, and a memorial at the Wounded Knee Massacre site. When Tamara begins a project for a tribal community she invites everyone to come together to share their thoughts about the new space. She lets them know that this is their building and that their vision and feelings matter. A new building involves the whole community because a school may also be a community center or gathering space. Tamara's reputation of listening has allowed her to become a trusted architect for native communities.

Tamara is an advocate for indigenous architects and dedicated to her role with American Indian Council of Architects and Engineers (AICAE). She often collaborates with schools encouraging students to be involved and active within their native communities early on. She realizes her role as an inspiration to young girls and Native Americans and often speaks at schools and graduations. It was during her education in college where she felt as though being Native America was the biggest challenge. She felt as though other students did not understand her culture and held on to stereotypes. It was professionally where she felt her gender got in the way more. She had to prove to the builders that she was the one they should be speaking with regarding the project. There is still work to be done and fortunately trailblazers like Tamara Eagle Bull are out there making a difference.

Evolution of the chair from

| COLONIAL | FEDERAL | VICTORIAN |

Ladder back chair first introduced in the 17th century. The back consisted of 2-6 slats. The seat was made with rush which is long grasses twisted together. The back of chair resembles a ladder often made from hardwoods

Duncan Phyfe (1810-20) chairs had different motifs on the back, shown here is a lyre (string instrument) motif. Chair legs end in animal feet. Designs were delicate and emoted grace and sophistication. Upholstery was introduced which added comfort, color and pattern.

Victorian chairs have ornate detailing. Chairs had spindles on the back and arms. Often with upholstered arms, back and seat. Brass casters were added for mobility. Victorian furniture had a look of heaviness with intricate detail and dark woods.

| MODERNISM | POST-MODERN |

The Bibendum Chair designed by Eileen Gray in 1926. Geometric design with minimal detailing. Shiny metal, unconventional shapes and often using muted colors were some characteristics of art deco furniture

The Isokon bentwood chaise lounge chair designed in 1930 by Marcel Breuer began production in 1960. Modernism began to explore organic shapes and connect the shape of the human body to the design of the furniture.

The Bel Air Armchair design my Peter Shite in 1982. Highlighting asymmetrical design, bold colors and unexpected geometry. Memphis was a design style during post modern that was not shy with color and pattern.

Colonial to the present

In 1830 the Thonet Brothers developed a technique to steam wood in a pressure chamber in order to bend it. This came to be known as "bentwood" furniture. The industrial time lead to new manufacturing abilities and innovation.

The Gustav Stickley chair designed in th early 1900's. A heavy oak chair focusing on craftsmanship. Arts & crafts furniture was simple with clean lines, it was durable using solid wood for construction. This was a reaction to the over detailed furniture from the past.

The Barcelona chair designed by Ludwig Mies van der Rohe in 1929. Sleek elegant designs. Chrome and leather added to its sophistication. International furniture was simple and had no reference to historical styles from the past.

Desinger Verner Panton created the Panton chair in 1959. The postwar time in Europe brought plastic to the scene. Plastic polymer could be molded into almost any shape. This cantilevered design was new and exciting.

The Wiggle Chair designed in 1968 by Frank Gehry. Furniture becoming art pieces in a space. The Wiggle chair is made from a cardboard material. Deconstructivism was about the manipulation of materials and shapes.

The UltraStellar chair designed by Zaha Hadid in 2016. Made from American walnut. Defies what seems possible with wood. Complex craftsmanship and blending of materials. The evolution of the chair will continue...

Neri Oxman

As a young girl, Neri grew up in Haifa, Israel with her American father and her Israeli mother. Her home was full of creative energy. Her parents were often researching and designing and were very involved in the local design scene. After completing her mandatory military service in Israel, Neri went on to begin her pre-medical studies preparing herself to become a medical student. It wasn't long until she changed course to study architecture. Initially she attended the Technion-Israel Institute of Technology, ultimately completing her degree at the Architectural Association in London. From London she made her way to Cambridge, Massachusetts and earned her PhD at MIT in Design Computation. Neri has not followed the traditional route of going from architecture degree to practicing architecture. Her focus on design computation is about her passion for the development of alternative design solutions to social or ecological design challenges. Neri is a multidisciplinary architect blending inventor, scientist, educator and engineer all into one.

Neri is the pioneer of the field of Material Ecology, where she uses biology to inform materials and solutions to the built environment. She is a professor at MIT and the founder of the Mediated Matter research group. She and her team study the connection of nature, human biology and the future, letting the buildings work with and repair Mother Nature and in turn letting nature build the buildings.

In 2015 she developed a revolutionary process to 3D print glass. This glass can be used at an architectural scale, as it can be printed in ways that affect its thermal properties and solar transmittance. In other words, she can control how much heat, cooling and light go through the glass and is working on ways to create printed glass that can harness or gather solar energy. This is an example of a building potentially benefiting our environment and reducing the effect of global warming. When you think of biology, nature and the built environment as an ecology, you can work towards blurring the lines between nature and artificial elements.

We are in a time where resources are drying up and human-made products are taking over nature. Neri believes that the relationship between nature and humanity needs to be rebuilt and work together. This is a shift from human-centered design to nature-centered design. Neri's innovative thinking that continues to challenge where we are architecturally and where we can go is not only groundbreaking, it is our future.

In 1979 Frida Escobedo was born in Mexico City. From a young age she loved the arts. Frida's father was a doctor and she would go with him to work at the hospital. She would stare out the windows at the town below, a distant observer of the lives around her. Wondering how people used their spaces, how do those spaces reflect who is living inside. When it was time to set off to university Frida was too shy to study fine arts. She was not willing to display her emotions and express herself to others through her art, so instead she chose to study architecture. From the moment she started studying she loved it! She knew she chose the right path. After earning her bachelor's degree in Architecture and Urbanism from the Universidad Iberoamericana in Mexico, Frida worked for a short time before continuing her education. In 2003 she received a master's degree in Art, Design and the Public Domain from the Harvard Graduate School of Design. After graduation Frida returned to Mexico City and started her own design studio at the young age of 26.

In 2018 she was the youngest architect and second female architect asked to design the Serpentine Pavilion in London. The pavilion is a temporary installation in Kensington Gardens and its goal is to provide a multi-purpose space for people to gather and interact with contemporary art. Thrilled and anxious about the opportunity, Frida studied Mexican architectural vernacular to inspire her design, resulting in a journey of enclosed courtyards similar to traditional Mexican homes. For materials she used traditional English roof tiles in an innovative unexpected way. This project earned her many accolades from the public and her peers.

Frida's work spans projects ranging from residential to hospitality to public spaces. She challenges herself to keep things simple in shape and form. Among her many accomplishments, Frida was one of 32 architects asked to develop a prototype for an innovative community development project in Hidalgo, Mexico. The goal was to develop affordable housing for Mexican workers and improve their living conditions. In 2022 Frida was invited as one of five architects to be part of a five month competition to design the new modern and contemporary wing for the Metropolitan Museum of Art in New York City. Frida was selected and will be on a seven year journey to create a new vision for the museum.

Frida's commitment to her community, the architectural process, and innovation is inspiring. With a long journey ahead, her designs will continue to put her in the spotlight where even a shy girl from Mexico can thrive.

"Architecture shapes the world we live in
Good architecture is good life."

Emma Miloyo

Emma was born and raised in Nairobi, Kenya. She attended Kenya High School and then went on to study architecture at Jomo Kenyatta University. Emma was an only child raised by two very strong women, her mother and her grandmother. Her mom was a math teacher at Kenya Science Teachers College and was one of very few female faculty members. She always encouraged Emma to push the boundaries of the roles and expectations for women. Emma's grandmother was a powerful role model for Emma as she grew up. She was a successful farmer and worked hard for her accomplishments. At university Emma was a standout student. In 2006 she was the first woman to graduate with first-class honors in architecture. Emma worked for a few years after graduation. In 2009 she joined the firm Design Source in Nairobi. Emma is currently an architect and partner at the firm working alongside her partner. Emma has worked on a variety of projects from education to healthcare and religious and government projects. Her firm prides itself on putting the client first and listening to their needs. Not only is Emma committed to architecture that serves her community, she has always been an advocate for young girls. "Her lifelong ambition is to inspire young girls and help them break the glass ceiling that has limited their success, especially in male-dominated fields like architecture." Emma is a mixed race African woman in a sea of African men. In 2011 and 2018 she was recognized as one of the "Top 40 under 40 Women in Kenya" and in 2016 was named among the five Emerging Female Architects of East Africa by Archinect.com!

In 2017 Emma was selected as the first female president of the Architectural Association of Kenya (AAK), which has over 90% male membership. She believes that every situation is an opportunity. The industry is male dominated and being that there are fewer women it means they can stand out. In leadership people notice you and your are given a platform and that platform can be used in ways to encourage people to listen. Emma's advice is to "Speak loudly and speak on issues." Her role as president came at a critical time to work on gender roles in the industry. Her leadership has inspired more women to get involved and become leaders in other professional associations. She believes everyone deserves to be heard and have a chance to participate in the conversation. Emma is the co-founder of the Kiota School in Nairobi, which provides a safe and nurturing environment for children to learn and thrive. Emma's influence is present and her leadership and goals are making a difference. Emma is an architect, mentor, mother, wife, business owner, volunteer and educator. One woman can do it all, one day at a time, with a vision driven by her passion.

Glossary of Terms

adaptive reuse: taking an existing structure and adapting it for a new use

American Institute of Architects, AIA: the professional organization for architects

Beaux Arts: Architecture and design using historic forms and details, it is the teaching of architecture in France in the late 19th century.

Bernard Maybeck: American architect and professor known for his work in California

BFA: Bachelor of Fine Arts a higher education degree

chintz: A fabric/textile with lots of colors, often floral patterns, used in curtains and upholstery.

Cranbrook Academy of Art: a top art, architecture and design university in Michigan.

Eliel Saarinen: Finnish architect who influenced American modern architecture.

equality: each individual or group is given the same resources or opportunities

equity: everyone is provided with what they need to succeed, different for different people

Frank Lloyd Wright: American architect known for his "Prairie" style., he was a writer and theorist.

Gestapo: the secret police of Nazi Germany

Jane Drew Prize for Architecture: named in honor of Jane Drew, who was an advocate for women in a male-dominated profession

Ludwig Mies Van der Roche: German/American architect known for his contribution to International style and modern architecture and design

Marcel Breuer: Hungarian architect and designer known especially for his modern furniture

monolithic: large or massive forms, created from a single form or material

Pritzker Prize: an annual award that celebrates architects for their talent, vision and dedication to the field of architecture

Royal Gold Medal: an award given to a person or group who has influenced the advancement of architecture

social living: homes or apartments designed for low income people or families.

solar transmittance: the measure of light that passes through a piece of glass

thermal properties: how much heat passes through a material

toile: from the French saying "Toile de Jouy" a pattern that often includes floral or outdoor scenes it was popular in the Art Nouveau period

UNESCO: The United Nations Educational, Scientific and Cultural Organization, an agency that promotes international peace through education arts sciences and culture.

vignette: a collection or set up of objects and furniture to create a moment or a scene in a space

visual merchandising: the process of using light, color and material to create a retail display that attracts a customer

Walter Gropius: German/American architect who was a pioneer in the modern era and a founder of the Bauhaus school

meet the illustrators

Each of the illustrators are current or past students of the Interior Architecture program at Endicott College.

why students?

As a graduate student of Interior Architecture at New England School of Art and Design at Suffolk University, my Professor Jeanne Kopacz wrote the book "Color in Three-Dimensional Design." She asked to use my projects in her book. It was incredibly rewarding to be published in a book as a student; not only did it build my confidence, it was an amazing opportunity. I would like to pay it forward and give that same opportunity to my students.

Including students and alumni from Endicott College in this project is incredibly meaningful to me. I want to thank them for the inspiration and motivation they give me as a woman, mother, and professor. To be better, to do better, to stand out and to make a difference.

One of these women might just be the next groundbreaking architect or designer.

Paige Liljegren

Endicott 2015
Illustrator: Candace Wheeler

What was your favorite course in college and why?

I loved Studio the most. It allowed you to take the same problem as everyone else, and come up with anything you wanted to push your creativity. I think junior year is really where I started to understand who I was as a designer and had the technical skills behind me to make my vision come to life in concept, plans, and renderings.

What struggles have you faced on your journey to become a designer?

It's easy to get caught up in the details, and let those feelings become overwhelming. As designers, we are so passionate about what we do and what we are trying to say, so when we feel like something is in our way or not working out, it's a challenge to overcome that feeling. On the other hand, when you do figure out a way to make it happen, it's that much more rewarding of a feeling. I believe that's why design is a passion and a career, because if you don't have passion to persevere when challenges arise, then your design isn't going to be as successful.

Madison Pelletier

Endicott 2025
Illustrator: Louise Blanchard Bethune

Why did you want to be a part of this book?

I wanted to be a part of this book to not only have the opportunity to share my artistry with a larger community, but to portray one of the design world's historical female architects for future generations to see. The stories of these women are what made it possible for me to be studying design, I hope to have served them justice in my art piece.

What space have you visited that impacted you through design?

One place that has impacted me through design would have to be Ireland, more specifically the cathedrals and castles that I visited there. The traditional architecture is stunning and timeless, it really catches your eye from far away and reveals its true details when you get a closer look. Not to mention the original stained glass windows on some of the buildings are truly mesmerizing in person.

Gianna D'Aprile

Endicott 2020, MA 2021
Illustrator: Elsie de Wolfe

When or how did you know you wanted to be an interior designer?

Like most designers, I found myself at a young age drawing my bedroom layout in the sand at recess. But it wasn't until senior year of high school that my art teacher recommended interior design to me. My best subjects were math and art, and interior design seems to be a perfect mix of the two.

What was your favorite course in college and why?

In college I really enjoyed my Media III Rendering class. We used various medias to render spaces by hand. It was such a nice break from CAD/Revit® and it doubled as a therapeutic escape, where I could put music on and draw for the day.

Why did you want to be a part of this book?

Now that I am an adjunct professor, I would love to help educate young girls on different role models they can look up to in the design industry. There is a severe lack of female representation in the history of architecture and design, so bringing these influential women to the forefront would help tremendously. I also always hoped there would be a way to combine my two crafts and this opportunity seems like it accomplishes exactly that.

Who is your role model?

During my senior year of high school, my art teacher became a strong mentor for me and although I was not very confident in my work, she pushed and inspired me to enter a project in the Congressional Art Competition. My piece was chosen as the winner and was placed in the Capitol Building in Washington, DC for a year. This experience showed me the value of a role model and if it were not for my teacher's support and direction, I strongly feel that I would not have had the confidence to take the path that I did and continue with my art in college.

Sara Nobes

Endicott 2019, MA 2020
Illustrator: Marion Mahony Griffin, Neri Oxman and Florence Knoll

What are you passionate about when it comes to design?

Every opportunity to design is a chance to create something new, unique, different. A design project may range in budget and schedule to the next, but creativity is always present. Can I explore a new concept? Use a material in an unexpected way? Exploring new ideas and pushing my own creativity drive my passion for design.

When or how did you know you wanted to be an interior designer?

I owe it all to Lincoln Log®. I developed a love for creating & building while building Lincoln Log fortresses with my brother as a child. As I graduated to LEGO®, I honed my skills in picking up on the details and began recreating my bedroom.

Kaitlin Desbiens

Endicott 2016, MA 2017
Illustrator: Julia Morgan

What are you passionate about when it comes to design?

I am passionate about space planning and rendering. I love the puzzle-like, mathematical arrangement that space planning requires, offering clients with multiple possibilities of how to arrange their space that best fits them. I love how every way is unique and no two designers will think alike completely. The rendering phase offers that visual satisfaction of what the space could become, seeing how all the design choices along the process finally come together.

What was your favorite-course in college and why?

I enjoyed studio but my favorite course had to be electronic media and my rendering courses. Creating the visuals for a project in artistic ways was alway my favorite part, especially since everyone's style was always so unique. It allowed me to really be creative and not limit myself by the constraints of the 3D programs. It always helped to amplify my final project, making me feel truly proud of my work.

Amber Vuilleumier

Endicott 2020, MA 2021
Illustrator: Dorthy Draper & Sunita Kohli

Samantha Eisenbud

Endicott 2014
Illustrator: Eleanor McMillen Brown and Tamara Eagle Bull

What space have you visited that impacted you through design?

The Colosseum in Rome. Just standing outside the building alone with the immense amount of history associated with it is enough to excite you. But when you enter and feel the scale and complexity of the building- especially before the convenience of modern construction- it is inspiring. You can be face to face with an intricately detailed column capital that has survived nearly 2000 years. I love texture and layers in design and this building has them both in materiality and history.

Why did you want to be a part of this book?

I really loved my time at Endicott. I made incredible friends and mentors and was able to really begin developing my professional design skills. It is where I found my passion for hospitality design and was given the opportunity to study it further through a minor. Because of the internship program I was fortunate to get a head start in my career and quickly start applying everything I had learned. All of this has helped me grow to the professional I am today. It felt like a great opportunity to give back to a school and a professor who gave me so much.

Aleksandra Tsangarides

Endicott 2022
Illustrator: Margarete Schütte-Lihotzky and Odile Decq

What was your favorite course in college and why?

My favorite college course was called Florence Sketchbook, and I took it when I studied abroad in Florence, Italy. I've always been fond of creating in sketchbooks because of how intimate and personal they are, like artist diaries. This class was so amazing because I was able to explore hidden corners of the city and draw the beautiful sites around me every single day.

What are you passionate about when it comes to design?

I am most passionate about environmental issues and sustainability in design. Art and creativity has the power to speak to people in ways that words simply cannot. As an artist, I feel that it is my responsibility to share my experiences and knowledge of the natural world with other people so that we can all come together and fight for a healthier future.

Michaela Ellison

Endicott 2022
Illustrator: Beverly Loraine Greene

How would you describe your design style?

Describing and identifying design styles are one of my favorite things about interior design. Many of my colleagues have such a unique and artistic take on their work, that we joke we'd be able to identify each other's designs without needing a name on the project! When it comes to my design style personally, I'd say I'm very colorful. Every project of mine has a color palette that is utilized throughout the design harmoniously to suit my intentions of stimulation in a space. One of the best compliments I ever received from a colleague was her admiration that I'm not afraid of color, and I keep that as encouragement to try new things and break barriers.

What space have you visited that impacted you through design?

During my time studying abroad in Florence, Italy, I had the opportunity to visit the St. Peter's Basilica in Vatican City, Rome. I had studied the Basilica the previous year, so I knew the general idea of what it would look like. However, my expectations were blown away once I entered the Basilica. The marbling, imagery, sculptures, colors, and detailing almost had me in tears. Being able to walk through a space that I admired from books and photographs is something I will cherish forever. The impact of the St. Peter's Basilica pushes me to dream big for my designs.

What era would you have loved to be a designer and why?

I would have loved to be a designer in the late 19th and early 20th century, in the era of the Beaux Arts. Those buildings are "transformational," they provide an experience and allow their users to imagine themselves in an alternate reality somewhere far away in the past.

What advice do you have for the next gen. of architect or interior designer?

This field can be whatever you decide it is, let your passions guide you and craft pursuits that support them.

Yianna Buterbaugh

Endicott 2023
Featured Illustrator: Norma Merrick Sklarek, Frida Escobedo and more

What are you passionate about when it comes to design?

My favorite course in college was Electronic Media II, which I had with Professor Bischoff. In this class we learned Adobe Illustrator and were asked to create a textile design using the software. I not only enjoyed the creative process of creating a fabric, but also was inspired that my skills as a designer could transfer across many fields of design. It was also an opportunity to strengthen my relationship with Professor Bischoff, who was also my advisor at Endicott. I was really thankful for this relationship at school because she constantly offered support and was always creating or making us aware of all the opportunities in front of us.

Why did you want to be a part of this book?

I have been interested in illustrating for this project since she told me about it almost two years ago. While I learned how important a role women played in the development of art and design through the curriculum at Endicott, this role still gets overlooked in society at large. I was excited at the prospect of participating in a project that will create space to celebrate these women who often get overshadowed by their male counterparts.

Isabel Davern

Endicott 2021
Illustrator: Barbara D'Arcy

When or how did you know you wanted to be an interior designer?

Believe it or not, my 5th grade yearbook states, "When I grow up I want to be... an interior designer". My career was greatly influenced by watching my dad being a builder and maker my whole childhood, and still to this day. I also vividly remember a class project where I created my "dream home" - it had a waterslide going from my room to the infinity pool and my bed was made of cotton candy. The feeling that I was supposed to be creating stayed with me growing up, and I was lucky enough to always know the answer to that question.

What are you passionate about when it comes to design?

There are so many elements in our lives that we cannot control, and design gives us the ability to manage one thing, our environment. The spaces we pass through everyday directly affect one's happiness, energy, productivity, interactions, and overall health. Every space we enter stimulates a reaction, even if just subconsciously. Most importantly these surroundings shape meaningful experiences and memories. Many may not realize that designers have a major impact on the human quality of life. It is an incredible superpower we get to hold.

Julia Ferraro

Endicott 2019
Illustrator: Beverly Willis and Sheila Bridges

Lindsey Arthur

Endicott 2017 MA 2018
Featured Illustrator: Denise Scott Brown, Zeynep Fadıllıoğlu and more!

When or how did you know you wanted to be an interior designer?

My design journey began at a young age. I was fortunate to be raised in a family that encouraged my creativity, self-expression and independence. I was given the opportunity to find my own voice and discover my passion for creating, designing, crafting and helping others. I chose interior design as my career path because it allowed me to combine all that I love to do. Through design, I create spaces and utilize materials and objects in ways that express my design aesthetic and offer, to those who inhabit and use the space, a sense of peace, beauty, functionality and purpose.

Why did you want to be a part of this book?

I want to be a resource, and a voice, for young girls. I want to be part of something that empowers others to strive, dream, and create. This book is an opportunity to do this. The world will push us in many directions, give many opinions, and perhaps ignore or disregard what we are expressing and offering. But we must discover the voice within and find our own way of creating; that is how we grow and that is how we change the world. None of us should ever allow someone else's ideas or judgments to stop us from seeing, believing, creating in our own way. Each of us can do anything that we set our mind to...even that which seems unimaginable.

Madison Demberg

Endicott 2022, SCAD 2024 MFA
Themed Entertainment Design
Illustrator: Susan Maxman

What space have you visited that impacted you through design?

My home. I could name cathedrals, monuments, museums, and mansions full of color, and architectural features that fill the pages of my textbooks, but home is where it started. Growing up painting my room, changing the layout, and filling the walls, I was able to make it my own world. My love for design grew at home. My mom decorated the house filling it with countless memories, birthdays, movie nights, Christmas mornings, etc. Years went on and the house was repainted, rearranged, and improved. It grew with us. Our homes hold memories and emotions. This inspired my love for design. To be able to create a space where memories are made.

What are you passionate about when it comes to design?

When it comes to design, we as designers have the power to affect those around us and cause change, people are affected by their environments and designers have the ability to control that. I have always been fascinated by how the space around you can affect your mood and emotions. As a designer, I have the ability to create spaces for the well-being of others. I have the ability to create a memory.

Sydney Kimball

Endicott 2018
Illustrator: Clodagh

What advice do you have for the next gen. of architect or interior designer?

I would like young girls to know that interior design and architecture are more intertwined than people perceive them to be. Getting to have a career in this field is always exciting. No two projects are ever the same and neither is a day of work. Some days I'm in the office, others I'm on a construction site. Sometimes I spend my days drawing plans and others are spent presenting finishes to clients. No matter what the day brings, I always have pride in the work I get to do..

When or how did you know you wanted to be an interior designer?

I don't think there was ever a time I didn't have an interest in architecture and design. I was always interested in how buildings and spaces were designed and constructed. Even as a young kid, I was playing with LEGO® or using a house building simulation computer game. Any medium I could use to get my ideas across to others.

What are you passionate about when it comes to design?

I think when it comes to design I am the most passionate about creating a well functioning space. I definitely spend a lot more time on the space planning phase than any other. In high school I was in a lot of math and science courses and I think that is why the space planning and creating functionality within the space is where I thrive.

When or how did you know you wanted to be an interior designer?

I think I actually knew this early on in life however it didn't really hit me until I was a junior going on college tours. Growing up I was always fascinated by renovating and reorganizing spaces and would always help my dad in any way I could when he was up-keeping our house as well as my grandmother's. I didn't consider this as a career path until Junior year when I was convinced I would go into some sort of science degree. When I visited Endicott I just fell in love with the campus and the program fascinated me in more ways than I expected and then I knew this was the path for me.

Jessica Dubois

Endicott 2020
Illustrator: Yasmeen Lari

What advice do you have for the next gen. of architect or interior designer?

My advice is to focus less on trends versus timelessness. Focus more on genuine human connection and what we need from our spaces. Spend time with your mind thinking of interesting connections and researching new ways to create instead of just repeating what others have done.

What struggles have you faced on your journey to become a designer?

My journey to being a designer has not been anything that I planned. It has been confusing and scary at times and becoming a content creator felt like giving up my previous self. However, I have learned to embrace change and I feel as though my current career was made uniquely and perfectly for me.

Emily Shaw

Endicott 2020
Illustrator: Zaha Hadid and Karen Braitmayer

What was your favorite course in college and why?

My favorite course in college was environmental psychology. I loved learning about the relationship between our environment and our physiological well being. It emphasized my passion for interior design by marrying my two favorite things, the human experience and design.

What are you passionate about when it comes to design?

I believe that we are a mosaic of all the people, places and experiences we have ever encountered. As a designer I am passionate about the idea that we have the ability to design spaces that facilitate memories and experiences that add to someone's mosaic.

Maeve Kelly

Endicott; 2019
Illustrator: Maya Lin

Jillian Hersey

Endicott 2023
Illustrator: Jeanne Gang

What space have you visited that impacted you through design?

As an interior architecture major, everywhere I travel I find beautiful architecture and unique interior design inspiring. I have traveled to New Orleans and fell in love with the colorful buildings and decorative wrought iron railings of the French Quarter. Studying abroad in Florence, Italy gave me opportunities to visit countless ancient pieces of beautiful architecture and design from Italy, Greece, England, and France. Each location has brought me something different to draw inspiration from.

Why did you want to be a part of this book?

Reading is a strong passion of mine. I get lost in the words and pictures of every book that captures my attention. A book about female empowerment, women supporting women, as well as current and past interior designers and architects is the first book I would buy because it stands for everything I believe in as well as my passion for interior design. Inspiring a young girl to work toward her passion for interior design and architecture would be the greatest gift I could ever receive.

Lauren Bower

Endicott 2020, MA 2022
Illustrator: Emma Miloyo

What advice do you have for the next gen. of architect or interior designer?

I would say to own it. This industry is predominantly male driven and I know it can be hard sometimes when it feels like people are not taking you seriously but that is even more of a reason to work hard and show the world that women are just as good if not better and deserve to have a spot at the table in the architectural industry.

Who is your role model?

My role model is my mom. She has always pushed me to be creative and to be bold when situations may seem intimidating. She has been there through all of the failures and successes and I owe many of my accomplishments to her.

Ashlyn Young

Endicott 2021, MA 2022
Featured Illustrator: Design styles, chair evolution and color theory perspectives

When or how did you know you wanted to be an interior designer?

From an early age I've always loved everything art and design, but I didn't always know what I wanted to be when I grew up. For a long time, I thought I wanted to be an art teacher. However, when it came time to pick a college major on a whim I chose to pursue interior design. I thought to myself, "I change around my room every few months and I love HGTV maybe interior design would be fun". I fell in love with the major very quickly in college and soon realized this is where I was meant to be.

What era would you have loved to be a designer and why?

I would have loved to be a designer during the Art Nouveau era! When I was little, my dad went on a business trip to Barcelona, Spain. When he came home he gave me souvenirs and pictures of the beautiful Barcelona architecture. I was obsessed! Park Güell, Casa Batlló, and La Sagrada Familia were unlike anything my little eyes had seen before. From those pictures, Antoni Gaudí became my favorite architect. During my semester abroad I was able to visit Barcelona and experience all of Gaudí's work in person; pictures do not do them justice.

What space have you visited that impacted you through design?

I will never forget my first steps into the Pisa Cathedral in Italy. It's soaring ceilings literally took my breath away. I felt so small in the vast interior. The columns drew my eyes upwards and the space opened up above me. I will forever be grateful for my opportunities to study abroad in Florence and Milan. Seeing the slide show from my art history lecture class at Colby College in Waterville, Maine come to life right before your eyes is remarkable.

When or how did you know you wanted to be an interior designer?

As a child I was constantly drawing floor plans on graph paper of my dream homes. The grid of the paper kept me in line but the emptiness let me create. I will never forget the time my friend and I stayed up all night and built a one story doll house out of wood in my basement. It wasn't until later in life that I realized that not everyone can see spaces in plan and that maybe I had a gift.

Sarah Bischoff

BA Colby College, MFA NESAD
Endicott Professor 2012-present
Author and illustrator

DESIGN LIKE A GIRL

RESOURCES

The artwork and research for this book have been completed with passion and care. I would like to share the resourc[...]
that helped me complete this project.

ARCHITECTURE AND DESIGN RESOURCES
dailyartmagazine.com
architectuul.com
architectmagazine.com
archpaper.com
dezeen.com
beyondthebuilt.com
interiordesign.net
businessofhome.com
surfacemag.com
madamearchiect.org
pinupmagazine.org
curbed.com
designboom.com
architecturaldigest.com
the-modernist.org
atomic-ranch.com
indiadesignid.com
architectandinteriorsindia.com
stirworld.com
architectural-review.com
re-thinkingthefuture.com
surfacemag.com
aperature.org
archdaily.com

ORGANIZATIONS
greatnortherncatskills.com
pioneeringwoman.bwaf.org
The American Institute of Architects
National Institute of Building Sciences
Academy of Achievement
The Architectural Association of Kenya

NEWS AND PUBLICATIONS
The New York Times
The Seattle Times
The Philadelphia Inquirer
Saturday Evening Post
Bloomberg
npr.org
mascontext.com
newmobility.com
The Irish Echo
The New Yorker
Time Magazine
LA Times
The Guardian
pbs.org

LEARN MORE ABOUT THE WOMEN IN THIS BOOK
Candace Wheeler reference metmuseum.org
Louise Blanchard Bethune reference pioneeringwomen.bwaf.org
Elsie de Wolfe reference gardnermuseum.org
Sophia Hayden Bennett reference pioneeringwomen.bwaf.org
Marion Mahony Griffin reference pioneeringwomen.bwaf.org
Julia Morgan reference pioneeringwomen.bwaf.org
Dorothy Draper dorothydraperhome.com
Eleanor McMillen Brown mcmilleninc.com
Margarete Schütte-Lihotzky reference moma.org
Beverly Loraine Greene reference pioneeringwomen.bwaf.org
Florence Knoll knoll.com
Norma Merrick Sklarek reference pioneeringwomen.bwaf.org
Barbara D'Arcy reference fredericmagazine.com
Beverly Willis bwaf.org
Denise Scott Brown venturiscottbrown.org
Susan Maxman reference pioneeringwomen.bwaf.org
Clodagh clodagh.com
Yasmeen Lari heritagefoundationpak.org
Sunita Kohli sunitakohli.com
Zaha Hadid zaha-hadid.com
Zeynep Fadıllıoğlu zfdesign.com
Odile Decq odiledecq.com
Karen Braitmayer studiopacificaseattle.com
Maya Lin mayalinstudio.com
Jeanne Gang studiogang.com
Sheila Bridges sheilabridges.com
Tamara Eagle Bull Encompass Architects
Neri Oxman oxman.com
Frida Escobedo fridaescobedo.com
Emma Miloyo designsource.co.ke

SURVEYS
AJ Women in Architecture Survey
Architectural Review 2016 Women in Architecture Survey
2018 Equity in Architecture Survey
Narrow the Gap
Associate of Collegiate Schools of Architecture ACS

MUSEUMS
50yearsafterwhitneyyoung.org
metmuseum.org
moma.org

Printed in the USA
CPSIA information can be obtained
at www.ICGtesting.com
LVRC090730081123
763265LV00028B/985